Contents

This book provides the essential foundations for every young, aspiring gymnast. The author's extensive working knowledge of gymnastics and his vast experience of coaching the sport at all levels, are reflected in every chapter.

At the introductory level, gymnastics offers every youngster the opportunity to become physically literate and discover the joy of moving. At the highest level, gymnastics is one of the most demanding and exciting of sports. This book gives everyone, whatever their ability, the best possible start. It is an excellent text and one that will not gather dust on your shelf!

Sue Campbell
Director, The National Coaching Foundation

The increased popularity of gymnastics over the last decade or so has brought with it – as one might expect – a proliferation of publications riding the tidal wave of enthusiasm for this great sport. All but a few have dealt only superficially with the topic of preparing young physiques for the rigours of this demanding activity.

In setting down his own approach to the fundamental needs of gymnasts, Trevor Low has been able to draw upon a vast depth of knowledge from his own experience, firstly as talented schoolboy gymnast, progressing through the senior competitive field, and finally in the world of coaching and gymnastics journalism. His background embraces the whole spectrum of our sport.

The result is a most thorough handbook dealing with all aspects of gymnastics. Its thoroughness reflects Trevor's own philosophy, which has enabled him to coach many gymnasts to a high level of performance whilst at the same time paying attention to the personal needs and overall development of his pupils.

This book provides the coach with a sound scheme of work based on tried and tested practices, enabling the gradual build up of skills. Equally, however, it suggests how physical education teachers might develop their own programme of activity, utilising the step-by-step approach.

I would recommend this book as essential reading to all those involved with gymnastics coaching.

Bob Currier
Chairman, British Schools Gymnastics Association

A native of Dunfermline, Trevor Low became involved in gymnastics as a performer in 1966.

He holds the highest qualifications possible as a coach under the British Amateur Gymnastics Association awards system, and is currently coach to Hinckley Gymnastics Club in Leicestershire.

Trevor Low is editor of the *Gymnast* magazine and author of *The Technical Journal of Gymnastics*, a world-wide publication for teachers and coaches of gymnastics.

GYMNASTICS
Floor, Vault, Beam and Bar

TREVOR LOW

THE CROWOOD PRESS

First published in 1986 by
The Crowood Press Ltd
Ramsbury, Marlborough
Wiltshire SN8 2HR

Paperback edition 1993

This impression 1997

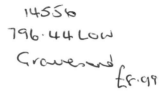

British Library Cataloguing-in-Publication Data

A catalogue record for this book is available from the British Library

ISBN 1-85223-752-X

Acknowledgements

The publication of any technical document is the result of many
years of research, experience and guidance. I have been
extremely lucky, having found early in my coaching career not
one, but two mentors who steered a clear path for me towards an
understanding of the skills of my craft. The first was the late
Harold S. Davies, champion gymnast and champion coach, who
taught me patience and showed me by his example the art of
teaching. The second was John Atkinson, from whom I came to
understand the meaning and method of motivation and
inspiration. To both my wise counsellors and friends, thank you.

My thanks too to Keith Holman, who spent many hours with me
ensuring that the sequence photography was both accurate and
complete, and to Eileen Langsley for the cover and action
photographs. Thanks also to the Leicester Mercury for the
photograph on page 1.

Typeset by PCS Typesetting, Frome
Printed in Great Britain at the Bath Press

Introduction

Over the past ten years gymnastics has emerged as one of the most popular sports to watch, both on television and live in the arena. Perhaps more than any other sport it contains many of those qualities which we most admire in human activity; strength, grace, courage, skill and excitement. As a sport it is the supreme test of ability. At the highest level in the Olympic games or the World Championships the difficulty of performance makes all other sports look easy. In the training-hall it is a sport which, like no other, offers an unlimited range of activities to learn. Even at the very beginning there are challenges and rewards as various skills and movements are encountered on the long road to the top. Each simple skill is a building block which helps the gymnast to

An instinct for gymnastics?

1

Introduction

construct complex movements. This book will explore the world of rolls and jumps, cart-wheels and handstands to help you discover those building blocks and use them to create your own exercises.

There are three types of gymnastics. Firstly, there is 'artistic' gymnastics which for men includes floor exercises, side-horse (or pommelled horse), rings, vault, parallel bars and the high horizontal bar. For women as well as the vaulting and floor exercises there are the beam and the asymmetric bars. Secondly, there is 'sports acrobatics' which is for men and women. Part of sports acrobatics contains the only section in which men and women appear together as a team. This branch of the sport relates much more closely to the type of acts still to be seen in the circus, but with very carefully organised rules to make it competitive. And finally there is 'rhythmic' gymnastics which is only for women. In a series of events, dance and simple floor exercises are combined with small hand apparatus such as, clubs, ribbon, rope, hoop or ball. Rhythmic gymnasts have a team event in which a selection of the hand apparatus is used. The first few chapters of this book are relevant to every type of gymnastics while the later sections go on to study in detail the most basic form of apparatus work for artistic gymnastics.

Before reading this book it is necessary to point out that all sports require great care and attention to detail. Any activity has its dangers if performed badly or in poor conditions. This book is your guide to understanding the basic movements of gymnastics and checking your progress with a logical and straightforward list of skills which are set in order of difficulty. This is not a DIY book of gymnastics. Only in an organised club or class with an experienced and qualified teacher will you be able to progress with success and safety. Use this book to learn about your sport. Knowledge is the first key to success, hard work is the second. Be prepared before you enter the gymnasium, know what you are going to do and know how to do it. There is a great deal to learn and much fun to be found in achieving the simple skills of gymnastics.

1 The Warm-Up

Each month, each week and each day our bodies pass through many stages of activity and rest, consciousness and sleep. Indeed it is now known that there are many stages or cycles, some lasting a year or longer, which all living things experience. You know that when you first wake up in the morning it takes a few minutes to become accustomed to the light and a few minutes to organise your mind. But after a wash and some breakfast you are ready for anything. In the same way as waking up from peaceful sleep to consciousness, there is a transition to be made from simple, everyday activity to the demands of sport. That transition is made by warming up. The function of the warm-up is to prepare the body to exercise and learn – without it the sporting body is not efficient.

GETTING WARM

The first and most important purpose of the warm-up is to raise the body temperature. Muscles work better when the body is a little hotter than normal and the blood is flowing freely. The best exercise to raise the body temperature is light and continuous movement. Simple jogging around a gymnasium or a game of 'chase' for five minutes will serve the purpose. Running on the spot is equally effective but less exciting. Skipping can be fun: boxers have used complex skipping patterns as both a warm-up and to improve lightness of footwork and co-ordination.

FINDING THE RIGHT WAVELENGTH

Training often takes place after a day's work when the mind is focused on many other activities. After the bus ride to the gymnasium and animated conversations with your friends and family, it is necessary to tune in to the training wavelength. During the warm-up you can relax after the problems of the day and begin to set your mind on to the task of taking total control of your body. You cannot perform to your very best while still thinking about television, homework, friends or records. Think carefully about each exercise of the warm-up and try to feel the improvement in your body. You must imagine yourself with straighter legs and extended ankles.

The warm-up should not leave you tired but it should be reaching every part of your body. Once you have raised the body temperature, lightly exercise the fingers and the wrists, the neck and the ankles. Follow this with the shoulders, the spine and the hips.

Warm and light exercise is then followed by stretching to the natural limits of the body. You should understand the difference between stretching to the natural range of the body and stretching beyond the natural limits of the tendons, muscles and joint movements. The body will perform best when at its best, never when less than at its working range or when pushed to working beyond its best.

Exercises to sharpen up co-ordination and rhythm will bring command of the body

Fig 1   Suppleness. A more elastic body can make many more shapes.

into play. A set warm-up with pre-deter-
mined repetitions and order of exercise is
ideal. Warm-up to music is even better. The
demands of a ballet type of exercise are
excellent though at times difficult for the new
gymnast to follow and enjoy.

THE EXTENDED WARM-UP

Beginners in gymnastics will need a much
longer period of basic exercise than the
experienced gymnast, and so the warm-up
is often extended to take in basic shaping
and light exercise designed to improve the
body's ability to adopt certain postures. This
is in effect light strength conditioning to gain
more control of the body's actions, for
instance lifting the leg or circling the arms.
Many teachers and coaches use an
extended warm-up to rehearse simple floor
skills such as forward rolls or cart-wheels
which have already been taught but which
are still not perfect.

Gymnastics is a sport which is guided by
rules which state how movements must be
done and how they must look. The appear-
ance of everything you do is very important
and so a great deal of time will be spent on
ensuring that the arms and the legs are in
the correct place during each skill and that
they produce pleasing lines.

WARM-UP 1

Raising the Temperature

There is no substitute for running. If you are at home, then the best way of getting warm is to put on your track suit and run around the block. Three or four minutes will be enough – this is a light jog not a race!

Fig 2   Running to warm up.

If you are at school, in a class or a club then it is much more fun to make up running games. Simple chasing games will ensure that everyone is warm after a few minutes. A forfeit of five press-ups when caught by the chaser can be a good motivation for being faster on the feet when rejoining the game.

Fig 3   A chasing game.

Loosening the Joints

The Fingers and the Wrists
(a)   Clench and unclench your fists 10 times.
(b)   Lock the fingers together and rock the clasped hands back and forth 10 times.

(c)   With the fingers still interlocked, turn the back of the hands to face the body then turn the palms of the hands to face the body. Repeat this 10 times.

The Shoulders *(Fig 4)*
(a)   Stand with feet apart, head held up. The arms are circled over the head and backwards, brushing the sides of the head as they pass. Repeat this 10 times circling backwards then a further 10 times circling forwards.
(b)   Now hold both arms out to the side at shoulder height. Keeping them at the same level, pull them backwards as far as they will go. This is also repeated 10 times.

Fig 4   Shoulder exercise.

The Hips *(Fig 5)*
(a)   Stand with feet apart and place hands on hips. Keeping the feet and the shoulders still, make 10 large circles with the hips.

Fig 5   Hip exercise.

The Warm-Up

The Spine *(Fig 6)*
(a) With feet apart and hands on hips, relax the spine allowing the chin to rest on the chest and the back to become round. Breathe out. Now lift the head to look at the roof and hollow the back with the chest pushing out. Breathe in. Each movement is to be done 5 times.
(b) On hands and knees on the floor, hollow the back and look at the roof. Next, round the back whilst looking at the chest. Complete 5 of each.
(c) From a kneeling and upright position with the hands behind the head, turn to look first to the right and then to the left. Keep the knees and the hips facing the front. 10 to be done for each side.

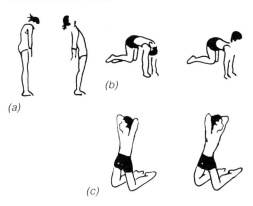

Fig 6 (a)–(c) Spine exercises.

The Ankles *(Fig 7)*
Much of the ankle joint will already have become very mobile during the running stages of the warm-up.

(a) In front support (press-up position) push the heels as far back as possible then forwards again. Push back 10 times.
(b) From a kneeling position, sit down on the heels and gently lift the knees off the floor. One set of 10 is to be done.

Fig 7 (a) and (b) Ankle exercises.

The Light Stretch

There are very few areas of soft body-tissue which do not respond to stretching. With time and hard work anyone can become supple. But there are very strict rules to stretching which must be followed.

1. The body must be warm and remain warm whilst the session is in progress.
2. Stretching is best performed in a relaxed atmosphere, slowly and gently. The body must not be tense during the exercise if it is to benefit.
3. There must be no forced stretching to start. Only qualified and experienced coaches will have the knowledge to use advanced methods of stretching.
4. There should be no bouncing actions employed. Stretching exercises are always a sustained and gradual pressure to create slow lengthening of the anatomy.
5. All stretching is uncomfortable and will produce stiffness and some pain for a day or so afterwards. It is vital therefore that stretching is introduced gently at first.
6. Most stretching will concentrate on the legs and the shoulders. Stretching and strengthening must progress together. Neglect neither. A balanced programme will ensure that you will become supple and strong in both the upper and the lower body (*see* Figs 8–9).

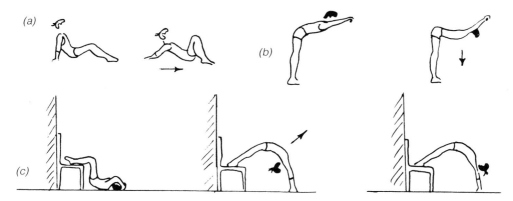

(a)

(b)

(c)

Fig 8 (a)–(c) Shoulder exercises.

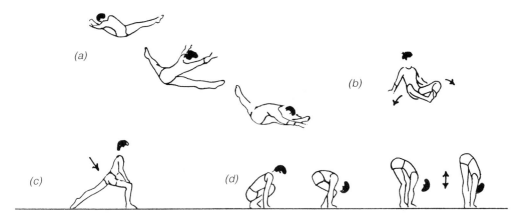

(a)

(b)

(c)

(d)

Fig 9 (a)–(d) Leg exercises.

Each exercise is to be repeated eight times with each position held for four seconds. Each stretching exercise should be performed with great care. Limbs must be straight where required – almost straight will not be good enough. Note the head positions indicated. It may not be possible to reach the shapes illustrated to start with, but remember that stretching is a progressive exercise and you will improve by just a little each time. It will be many weeks before you will be aware of this improvement, but success will come with determination and perseverance.

WARM-UP 2

This warm-up is far more advanced and complex in its structure. It begins as usual with an activity to raise the body temperature. In Figs 2–9 the gymnast is shown in leotard or shorts but of course the entire warm-up must be done wearing a good track suit or jogging suit. A high body temperature must be maintained throughout the warm-up and not lost after the first few exercises by taking off too much clothing.

Raising the Temperature

Running in a large gymnasium, normally in a circle, for a full minute, then the following variations:

(a) Continuing around the room in the same direction but side-stepping to face the centre.
(b) Side-stepping facing outwards, still moving in the same direction.
(c) Running forwards.
(d) Turning and running backwards.
(e) Running forwards.
(f) Running four strides and touching the floor with the right hand, then running for 4 strides and touching the floor with the left hand, 4 strides right, 4 strides left and so on.
(g) Running forwards.
(h) Running with the knees picking up very high in front.
(i) Running forwards then slowing to walk.
(j) Walking with the heels raised and the legs straight.
(k) Walking once more for a half minute to bring the breathing rate down a little.

Lower Body Exercises

The following exercises require a ballet bar, a beam or a box upon which to place the leg at a comfortable height.

Exercise 1 *(Fig 10)*
Adopt the starting position, and turn to face your leg. Reach down, pressing the chest on to the thigh for 8 counts. Hold the extreme position for 4 counts then lift the leg forwards and hold it out straight for a further 4 counts. Finally, release the leg and hold it out straight for 4 counts before swinging the leg 8 times from the rear to the front. Repeat with the other leg, stretching over to the other side.

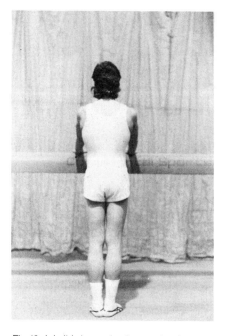 

Fig 10 (a)–(h) Lower body exercise 1.   *Fig 10 (b)*

Fig 10 (c)

Fig 10 (d)

Fig 10 (e)

Fig 10 (f)

Fig 10 (g)

Fig 10 (h)

Exercise 2 *(Fig 11)*
Adopt the starting position again. Note that in this exercise the arm is raised. Reach over and down with the shoulder on the thigh for 8 counts, then hold down for 4 counts. Lift the leg sideways for a hold of 4 counts then release and hold the leg upwards for 4 counts. Swing the leg to the side, keeping it straight for 8 counts. Repeat with the other leg, stretching over to the other side.

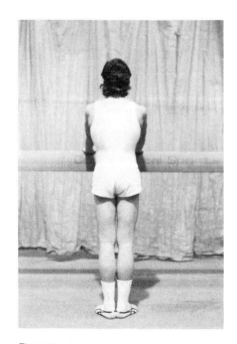

Fig 11 (a)–(g) Lower body exercise 2.

Fig 11   (b)

Fig 11   (c)

Fig 11   (d)

Fig 11   (e)

The Warm-Up

Fig 11 (f)

Fig 11 (g)

Exercise 3 *(Fig 12)*
Place the leg to the rear. Ensure that both legs are straight at the starting position. Bend the supporting leg 4 times, then reach upwards and backwards for a count of 4. Extend the leg high to the rear and hold for 4 counts before swinging it 8 times up to the rear.

Fig 12 (a)–(f) Lower body exercise 3.

Fig 12 (b)

Fig 12 (c)

Fig 12 (d)

Fig 12 (e)

Fig 12 (f)

Upper Body Exercises

Exercise 1 *(Fig 13)*

Press the shoulders down for 4 counts and then hold them down for another 4 counts. Hold on to the beam and pull the seat down to the floor for 4 counts then hold down for 4 counts. With the feet on the beam, perhaps held by an assistant, push the seat under the beam for 4 counts and then hold it under the beam for 4 counts. Once again with the feet on the beam, assisted if required, push the shoulders beyond the position of the hands 4 times, then with the legs straight hold the position with the head forced through for 4 counts.

Fig 13 (a)–(f) Upper body exercise 1.

Fig 13 (b)

Fig 13 (c)

Fig 13 (d)

Fig 13 (e)

Fig 13 (f)

Exercise 2 – Sunk and Extended Handstands *(Fig 14)*

Kick to a handstand either with support or against the wall and allow the shoulders to sink and relax. However, remember to keep the back straight. Extend out of the shoulders, lifting the handstand as high as possible. Repeat 20 times.

Exercise 3 – Dislocations with a Pole *(Fig 15)*

Use a wooden broom handle or a pole with a marked spot for the hand placements. Start in overgrasp with the bar at the front. Swing the pole carefully from front to rear, making a 'dislocation' with straight arms. Both shoulders must dislocate at the same time. Repeat 20 times. Each week draw the hands a little closer together and mark the new spot for the hands.

Figs 15 (d–e) show dislocations starting from the rear but in undergrasp. Make a further 10 dislocations ending in a handstand. Do not bring the bar to the front.

Fig 14 (a) and (b) Upper body exercise 2.

Fig 15 (a)–(e) Upper body exercise 3.

Fig 14 (b)

Fig 15 (b)

Fig 15 (c)

Fig 15 (d)

Fig 15 (e)

2 Fit for Gymnastics

More than any other sport gymnastics provides the individual with the ideal fitness profile. By this I mean that simple gymnastics will give a fine balance of muscular strength and endurance, stamina, a supple body and a well co-ordinated sense of movement and rhythm. Almost any gymnast can turn his or her hand to a wide range of sports very quickly and it is very common to find that good gymnasts are also excellent in other games. The gymnast will be in great demand at school for athletics, swimming, soccer, netball, hockey and so on. A few gymnasts are very lucky, starting out with a natural strength and a dynamic energy which is quickly spotted by a teacher or a coach. But for ninety-five per cent of children or adults entering the sport of gymnastics, fitness is produced only by a determined attitude to succeed and very hard work.

Fitness in gymnastics is often called conditioning and is divided into more specific types of work, each of which will improve some aspect of the physical condition of the body.

1. **Stretching.** This will improve the gymnast's ability to perform skills and as with the dancer, will allow him or her to create more shapes and lines.
2. **Strength.** This is made up of separate types of activity. The first is structure building, which exercises lightly, but often, the entire muscular frame of the body. Indeed, gymnastics exercises the parts that other sports cannot reach! The second category covers pure strength activities, which we all understand will give us the ability to lift heavier weights, chin a bar or kick a ball further. Muscular endurance, the third category, allows us to make more chin-ups or press-ups without feeling tired. The fourth category, that of dynamic power, is very important in gymnastics as many movements are performed at speed. The gymnast must exercise to have the explosive and accurate strength needed during complex routines.
3. **Stamina.** This is something which we usually relate to running games and sports.

Fig 16   Strength. Many positions require great strength and movements require powerful muscles.

Stamina is vital to the gymnast during floor exercises when the lungs have to work very hard to keep the oxygenated blood flowing to feed the energy system which helps keep the muscles working. Training for gymnastics as for any sport will require stamina fitness.

For simple gymnastics the beginner will find that a well-structured warm-up will provide ample exercise for the body, and, if followed carefully, will make a vital start to gaining the fitness required. Conditioning may be introduced a little at a time once the gymnast has already learned some basic movement patterns. It is important to remember that sport is fun but conditioning is painful. Those starting out in the sport seeking pure enjoyment may not accept happily the pain which results from exercise. However, those who are committed to learning, and are motivated through both achievement and enjoyment, will exercise to improve their fitness when presented with a well-balanced training schedule. Too great an emphasis on conditioning too early in the gymnast's career will be counter-productive. Six months spent building up interest and enjoyment will result in an eagerness to learn and an acceptance of the rigours of hard exercise.

Every exercise which is designed to help with the physical condition of the body must be learned correctly. For example press-ups by the thousand will benefit a gymnast very little if the wrong back shape is used. When first learning to exercise for strength and suppleness, always have an assistant or a partner with you who can tell you when something is wrong. Follow instructions carefully and with precision. You must always follow a set programme of work. A programme is a list of activities in a special order which tells you what to do, how to do it, when to do it, the number to be performed and often the time allowed for the exercise. An example is given below.

All conditioning is progressive. Someone who always does 50 press-ups each night will not become any stronger. Jogging for one mile each morning will not improve the stamina if the time taken is always the same, say 10 minutes. But if the time taken to jog that mile is less each day, even by as little as one second, this will show progress. Just one press-up added each week to the nightly exercise will make the arms stronger. For this reason you will now understand that conditioning must always be hard if improvement is to be made. Strength training always requires that extra effort, more determination and commitment. Often conditioning seems to show little result – after all, there is little difference to be seen between 50 press-ups and 51. The daily progress towards a good splits will be so small that it cannot be measured, but over a three month

Training Programme: Monday

Exercise	Instructions	Number	Time
Press-ups	With flat back, head still, arms bent 90 degrees	25, repeated twice	
Sit-ups	Feet held and legs bent, hands behind head	Maximum	1 minute

period there will be a noticeable improvement. But the exercise must be regular and organised. Haphazard and ill-prepared conditioning is of little value.

The following conditioning tables are just six of many which can be prepared. Two are for stretching exercises and four are for strengthening exercises. Variety is a great motivator so seek out additions to your exercise repertoire. There are many variations of the chin-up, each one using a slightly different combination of muscles and each one very effective. Always warm up the body before starting to condition. In a club or a school class, stretching will often take place immediately after the class warm-up and strengthening at the end of the training session. When exercising at home or on your own warm up before starting the conditioning programme. Small injuries such as pulled muscles are common when vigorous exercise starts when the body is cold. Never attempt to stretch after exercising for strength – it would have little effect and could cause injury. At the beginning of your gymnastics career, stretching once a week and exercising for strength twice a week will allow progress. After perhaps three months this can be increased to make progress more rapid.

(b)   Place the hands on wall-bars or a box at about hip height and press the shoulders down to the floor.

(c)   Using a stack of mats or a padded chair to find a comfortable position, lift up into a bridge.

(d)   Perform some dislocations with a broom handle held in both hands.

(e)   By holding on to a bar, or a beam, lower to the widest straddle stand possible without bending the legs.

(f)   From a sitting straddle position, reach down and through the legs, sliding the hands as far as possible forwards. Hold this position, then lift up trying to hollow the back to return to the starting position. At first this is a very difficult exercise to do and a very difficult position to reach. Progress towards the shape illustrated.

(g)   With one leg forward in a lunge, press the hips down to the floor. Keep the shoulders up and back.

(h)   Standing on a small box, reach down with straight legs and allow the body-weight to stretch the back of the legs.

(i)   Use a box or a bench to achieve a half-splits position. Now reach back with the hands and the shoulders. The back leg must be straight.

STRETCH PROGRAMME 1
(Fig 17)

These exercises can all be done by the gymnast alone, with the amount of stretch under his or her own control. They require the minimum of apparatus. Perform each 5 times, holding it for 8 seconds.

(a)   From a back support, bend the legs pulling the seat and shoulders away from the hands. Try to place the back on the floor.

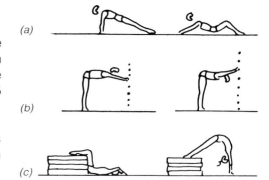

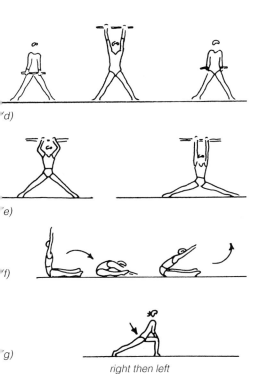

(d)

(e)

(f)

(g)

right then left

(h) (i)

right then left

Fig 17 (a)–(i) Stretch programme 1.

(a) From a position lying on the floor face down, the arms are pulled overhead and held close together by a partner.

(b) With support behind the shoulders, the arms are pulled back.

(c) While hanging on a bar, the shoulders are pushed up and forwards.

(d) A bridge is assisted by lifting the shoulders.

(e)–(h) (e) and (f) show the starting position with the feet raised and the legs straddled. Illustration (g) demonstrates how the partner pulls the arms until the chest is through the legs. To gain extra stretch a second partner can push from behind (h).

(i) The partner stands behind the kneeling gymnast and pulls one leg up whilst bracing the back on his leg.

(j) With two partners assisting, one leg is held down to the floor whilst the other is pulled over and down.

Note

Assisted stretching is not a game, and must be applied with common sense and skill.

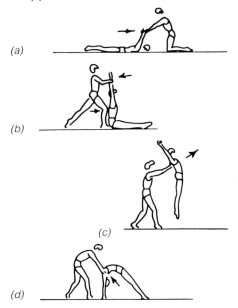

(a)

(b)

(c)

(d)

STRETCH PROGRAMME 2
(Fig 18)

This series of exercises requires the assistance of a second gymnast and should be supervised and taught correctly by an experienced coach. Remember that stretching exercises must never employ a bouncing action. Always use sustained and even pressure.

For the splits exercises stretch both legs. Repeat each exercise 3 times and hold it for 8 seconds every time.

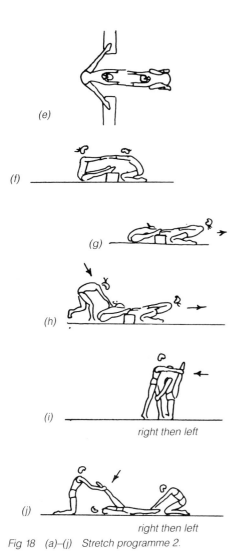

(c) Pull-ups on a bar. Pull as far as possible on the first few sessions (some assistance may be needed to begin with). Progress from 3 attempts towards making 8 full pull-ups.

(d) Press-ups with a straight body, seat tight. Progress from 5 attempts with assistance to 25 press-ups.

(e) Holding on to wall-bars or the top of a box, with your legs straight, extend the ankles to raise the body. Next, place the heels down, and bend the legs to 90 degrees before slowly straightening up. Repeat 10–25 times.

(f) Sprint runs for 25 metres (27 yards). These are best done outdoors. Start with 4 runs with 20 seconds rest between each run and progress towards 6 runs of 50 metres (54.5 yards) with 30 seconds rest.

Fig 18   (a)–(j)   Stretch programme 2.

STRENGTHENING CIRCUIT 1
(Fig 19)

(a) From a lying position sit up to a tucked position. Repeat 15–30 times.

(b) From a lying position face down, raise the arms, shoulders and legs from the ground keeping the seat tight. Repeat 15–30 times.

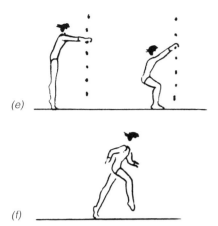

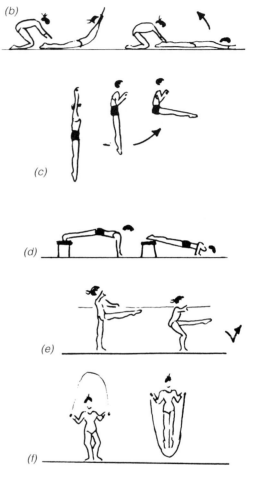

(e)

(f)

Fig 19 (a)–(f) *Strengthening circuit 1.*

STRENGTHENING CIRCUIT 2
(Fig 20)

(a)   From a lying position sit up to a V-position. Repeat 15–30 times.

(b)   From a lying position face down, with a partner holding down the legs, raise the upper body with the hands behind the head. Repeat 15–25 times.

(c)   Pull-ups to an L-shape. Each one is done slowly and from a still hang. Repeat 5–15 times.

(d)   Press-ups with the feet raised to shoulder height. Repeat 5–25 times.

(e)   Using a box or wall-bar for balance, with one leg raised make a half-bend with the supporting leg and then return to the original position. Repeat 12–30 times.

(f)   Skipping for stamina. Continue for 3 to 5 minutes.

Fig 20 (a)–(f) *Strengthening circuit 2.*

STRENGTHENING CIRCUIT 3
(Fig 21)

(a)   Hold a handstand against a wall for 30 seconds facing the wall and 30 seconds facing out.

(b)   Hold a straddle half-lever. Repeat 5 times, holding for 8 seconds each time.

(c)   While hanging lift the legs until the toes touch the bar. Repeat 6 times.

23

(d)   With a partner holding the heels, shoulders raise with the arms behind the head. Repeat 20 times.

(e)   On parallel bars, dips with straight body until the arms bend to 90 degrees. Repeat 12 times.

(f)   From a stand with feet shoulder-width apart and the arms straight, lift until the feet are just off the floor, then hold. Repeat 6 times, lifting and holding for 5 seconds.

(g)   Using benches or cardboard boxes, rebound stretch jumps. Perform 6 jumps repeated 5 times.

(h)   400-metre run timed. Each time the run is made the previous time should be beaten.

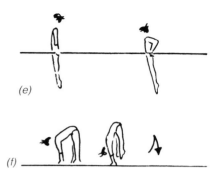

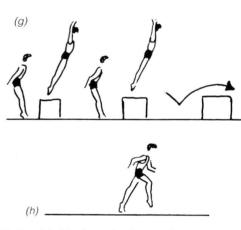

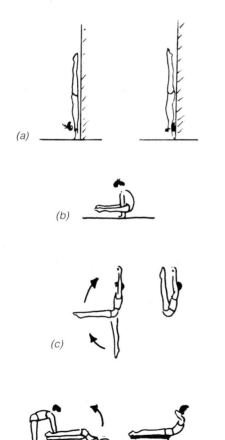

Fig 21   (a)–(h)   Strengthening circuit 3.

STRENGTHENING CIRCUIT 4
(Fig 22)

(a)   Heel raising repeated 20 times. Rebound jumps. From a back jump off a bench, perform a light jump from the back of the legs. Repeat 20 times.

(b)   For this the gymnast will need a small weight made from sand-filled socks. 20 leg extensions from a seated position. 20 heel lifts.

(c)   25 sit-ups to just touching the knees. 8 long sit-ups with an arched back. Sit-ups with a 90 degree turn, 10 to the right and 10 to the left.

lower leg

upper leg

stomach

back

upper arm

shoulder

handstand

stamina and endurance

and then

lift and press to handstand

(a)

(b)

(c)

(d)

(e)

(f)

(g)

(h)

(i)

Fig 22 (a)–(i) Strengthening circuit 4.

(d)   With a small weight held behind the head, rise up 15 times. Hold heels-up position 4 times for 10 seconds each time.

(e)   10 pull-ups with chin to bar. 10 pull-ups with back of head to bar. 12 dips, feet sliding. 12 dips with tuck.

(f)   While hanging, lift the shoulders backwards and hold 5 times for 5 seconds each time. Press shoulders forward and hold 5 times for 5 seconds each time. Shoulders forward then back, 8 times.

(g)   Handstand held for 1 minute. Sagging handstand against the wall, then straighten up and hold. Repeat 5 times with 5 seconds in handstand each time. Hold under pressure twice for 20 seconds each time.

(h)   Perform 10 squat jumps and follow this immediately with 10 press-ups, then 9 jumps and 9 press-ups, 8 jumps and 8 press-ups, 7, 6, 5, 4, 3, 2 and finally just 1 of each.

(i)   From straddle stand lift to handstand. Repeat 10 times. From headstand push to handstand. 8 times (with straight back).

3 Body Shapes

The first lesson of gymnastics is to learn the shapes into which the body can be moulded. For every skill or movement there is a defined shape which must be made. If that shape is not precise then the skill will be poorly performed. Some skills involve two or more shapes and can be very complicated. Understanding each shape is therefore vital to good gymnastics. Shape is the language of gymnastics; without the ability to express those shapes gymnastics can only be performed at a very low level. You should therefore spend a great deal of time learning the shapes and also discovering how to improve them by conditioning for a more supple and a stronger body.

Gymnastics is a spatial sport which not only involves movement in three directions, but also on many planes and in differing orientations. A shape can be made whilst standing, lying, sitting, inverted (upside-down), face down or on your side, and there are many more possibilities. From each of these variations the gymnast's view of the room changes, and awareness of where the floor is will change too. The gymnast must therefore learn to sense the plane which he or she is in by developing 'spatial awareness' – important later on as performing somersaults or twists will require a fine sense of spatial awareness for safety and success.

THE STRAIGHT POSITION
(Fig 24)

The straight position is achieved with the back as flat as possible, the seat tight and the head held upright. There can be any number of variations on the position of the arms but the body must be straight and there should be no loss of tension in the back.

Body tension is achieved by holding a muscle or group of muscles tight. Some muscles will have to be tight whilst others are relaxed. Try making a fist with one hand and relaxing the other or locking one arm rigid and straight whilst keeping the other relaxed. Alternatively, try to tighten the seat but leave both arms relaxed. You can invent many such practices to help you achieve body tension.

Fig 23   Versatility. The gymnast is a great all-round athlete. Gymnastics demands more qualities of activity than any other sport.

Body Shapes

Fig 24   The straight position.

THE TUCK *(Fig 25)*

The tuck is produced by drawing the knees up to the chest and placing the hands lightly on the knees. Do not clasp the fingers together or hold on to the legs behind the knees. The elbows should be held down and the head tilted forward with the chin close to the chest. Ensure that the ankles are extended.

Fig 25   The tuck.

THE PIKE *(Fig 26)*

A pike is a bend at the hip. There are two types of pike. The first is the basic pike which is an exact right angle of the body. The second is the closed pike, most often associated with the sport of diving, during which the fold of the body is so deep that the chest closes up to the thigh.

Fig 26   The pike.

THE DISH *(Fig 27)*

A complicated shape and a vital one for good gymnastics. To find this shape, begin by lying flat, face up on the floor. With the hands on the front of the legs make a short sit-up until the hands are nearly touching the knees. The back should be gently curved from the seat to the shoulder. Take care that the small of the back is also round. The arms can be extended in any direction once the back shape is found.

(a)

(b)

Fig 27   (a) and (b)   The dish.

THE HOLLOW AND THE ARCH *(Figs 28–29)*

These two shapes have been placed in one group so that the difference between them can be illustrated clearly. The hollow (Fig 28) can be achieved by lying face down and then lifting the legs and the chest from the floor. The weight is held on the mid-torso with the head held up. Once again the arms can be moved to a variety of positions without losing the hollow.

Fig 28   The hollow.

The arch (Fig 29) can be achieved by standing upright then, with the seat tight and the legs straight, raise the head to look at the

Fig 29   The arch.

Fig 30   The straddle.

ceiling whilst pulling the shoulders back to form a curve in the upper back. This in effect leaves the lower spine and the legs in a straight position and the upper spine hollow.

THE STRADDLE *(Fig 30)*

The straddle at its basic level is produced by opening the legs to about 100 degrees. Certainly 90 degrees or less will not constitute a straddle shape, and a greater angle than 100 degrees will at times make some skills more difficult.

Fig 31   Standing in a piked and straddled shape.

Fig 32 Sitting in a piked and straddled shape.

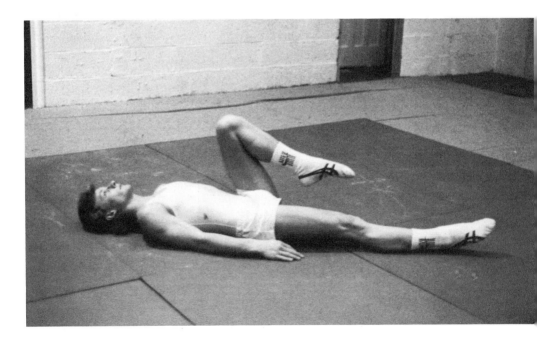

Fig 33 Lying with one leg tucked and the other straight.

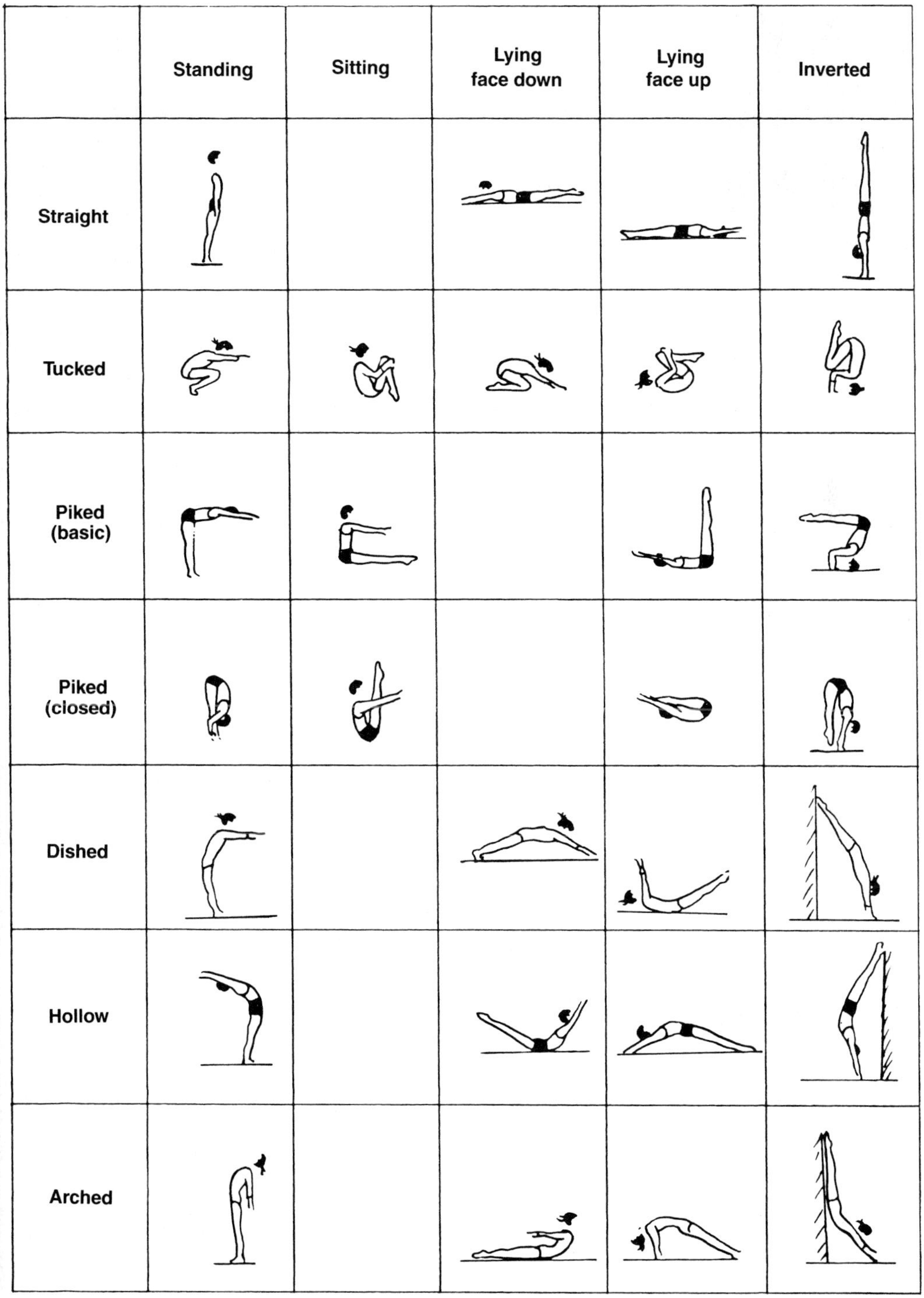

	Standing	Sitting	Lying face down	Lying face up	Inverted
Straight					
Tucked					
Piked (basic)					
Piked (closed)					
Dished					
Hollow					
Arched					

Fig 34   Some ideas for different shapes.

Fig 35   Inverted (upside down) position with a straight body, straddled.

VARIATIONS ON THE BASIC SHAPES

Variations using the arms and the legs can now be added to the repertoire of shapes (*see* Figs 31–35). With additional changes to the arm positions and by making the shape asymmetric (different parts of the body different shapes) the variety of positions is almost infinite. Remember to study the head positions.

4 Rolls

There is an old coaching joke which discusses the various rolls to be seen in the gymnasium, including sausage-rolls, Swiss rolls, ham rolls, salad rolls and so on. But there is only one forward roll – the right one, and from the outset you must understand that there is only one way of doing things in gymnastics. If the feet are not together in the forward roll or if the hands touch the floor more than once then it is wrong. More than any other sport gymnastics suffers from the unenlightened expert who encourages children to 'twizzle' and 'gambol', 'roly-poly' and 'flopsy'. It is very difficult to correct a fault once the body has learned it. It is much more sensible to learn everything correctly from the start.

Fig 36 Gymnastics is a great spectator sport.

FORWARD ROLL AND BACKWARD ROLL

Rolling is the most basic of the skills of gymnastics and comes from a common shape, the tuck. To put it very simply, round objects roll. From the basic tuck shape the spine becomes round and then the roll can begin.

Forward Roll *(Figs 37–42)*

To start the roll, lie in a tucked position and rock to and fro, building up the movement until the tuck is passing from the shoulders to the seat comfortably (Fig 37). At the beginning this demands great effort from the stomach muscles but the gymnast will improve rapidly. Keep the hands on the front of the knees as the roll increases. The temptation to use the hands for balance or to push the roll forward must be avoided.

Fig 37 Forward roll from tuck.

The next progression is to increase the roll until the tuck is brought forwards to be supported on the feet – a standing tuck (Fig 38). This should be practised until the feet can take the weight easily and smoothly.

Rolls

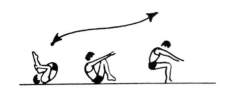

Fig 38.   Roll on to the feet.

Next, (Fig 39) starting from a position standing straight, crouch to a standing tuck then place the hands on the floor just in front of the feet. By pulling the head well forward on to the chest and giving a small push from the legs, roll over into a tucked shape, rocking to and fro.

Fig 39   Roll from a standing straight position.

Crouch down to a standing tuck, then roll back in a tuck, roll forwards again to a standing tuck and, swinging the arms upwards and forwards, rise to a position standing straight again. Encouragement to swing the arms forwards and upwards can be given by an assistant waiting to give a helping hand.

This completes the second part of the forward roll.

Fig 40   Roll into a standing tuck.

Clearly both parts of the simple forward roll can now be put together. This is made easier by the use of a small slope (Fig 41).

The roll can be improved by introducing a momentary pike part way through (Fig 42). This will improve the look of the roll and also increase the speed of the second part as the legs come into the smaller tuck from the pike. Once the body is moving, making it smaller makes it spin faster. This theory is often used in gymnastics and is vital when performing somersaults and advanced skills.

Fig 41   Forward roll down a slope.

Fig 42   Forward roll with pike.

Common Faults in the Forward Roll

1.   A flat back.
2.   Using the hands to push up at the end.
3.   With very young children, the arms are too short to make a roll with the head clear of the floor.
4.   Not being strong enough to hold the weight on the hands as the roll is tipped over.
5.   Feet wide apart as the gymnast rises.

Backward Roll (Figs 43–45)

The stages so far completed will also give the first half of the backward roll. From a position standing straight, crouch to a standing tuck before passing through a sitting tuck and rocking to and fro in a tucked shape. Rolling backwards requires rather more skill in the placement of the hands to support the weight as the body tips over on to the feet (Fig 43). Place the hands by the side of the head with the palms up and the elbows pointing forwards. Rocking to and fro in a tucked shape, try to touch the floor at the point when the shoulders are furthest back.

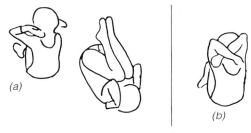

(a)

(b)

Fig 43   The correct hand placement for the backward roll.

Using a slope to assist the roll the following practice is excellent to give confidence. Sit at the top of the slope with the hands crossed behind the head. The right hand reaches over to the left shoulder across the back of the head and the left hand reaches to the right shoulder. This forms a strong and stable platform over which to roll. Then by rolling back the weight is tipped over easily to land on the knees. Progress from here to rolling back using the hands for support, then from stand to stand.

Fig 44   Backward roll from stand to stand.

Note that one of the most important technical features of the backward roll is that the weight is taken on the hands and the body is then pushed on to the feet. The tuck is held until the feet are on the floor, whilst the arms straighten as they push (Fig 44).

Common Faults in the Backward Roll

1.   Using the head as a support during the supported stage.
2.   Opening the tuck too early, preventing the roll from moving over the hands.
3.   Lack of push from the hands, resulting in the roll becoming stuck.
4.   Landing on the knees due to lack of push and arm extension.
5.   Failing to reach back for the floor early enough to make a worthwhile push.

The forward and the backward roll are the most basic of the simple gymnastics skills and yet they are quite complex in that the shapes must be formed at the right moment. Gymnastics *is* shape: keep the knees together in all these rolls and extend the ankles when they are off the ground. You will find that the shape with the feet turned up is less attractive (*see* Fig 45).

Fig 45   Correct and incorrect shapes.

Backward Roll into a Handstand *(Fig 46)*

This can be performed with straight or bent legs in the first stage. The gymnast must be able to perform a strong and straight handstand.

From a position standing straight, fold the chest down to form an open pike. Reach behind and lower yourself down into a seated pike. Reach back with the hands for the floor and roll the body back to an inverted pike. Stop the feet above the hands

Rolls

so that both the extension of the pike and the extension of the arms occur together, driving the body into a handstand or a straight inverted position.

Fig 46 Backward roll into a handstand.

Fig 47 Practice with assistance.

Note
The piked version is more suitable for boys than girls but the tucked backward roll into a handstand is more difficult to control even though it requires a little less strength.

Fig 48 Tucked backward roll into a handstand.

Forward Roll into Straddle Stand (Fig 49)

This skill causes many problems for young gymnasts as it does require a considerable range of movement to make a wide straddle and also some strength to push up to the straddle stand. However, looking at

the sequence of shapes within the roll, the skill can be seen to be less complex than at first thought.

(a) Begin from a position standing straight.
(b) Crouch down into a standing tuck.
(c) Using the hands for support, begin to roll into a lying closed pike.
(d) Roll over into a sitting closed pike with a straddle.
(e) Reach through very early with the hands to pass quickly through a sitting piked straddle.
(f) Bring the body into balance by passing the shoulders well forwards pushing off the floor with the hands between the legs.
(g) The skill ends with a straddle stand.

Note
A common fault often occurs when the gymnast straightens up too early, resulting in failure to bring the body into balance.

Fig 49 (a)–(g) Forward roll into straddle stand.

Fig 49 (b)

Fig 49 (c)

Fig 49 (d)

Fig 49 (e)

Fig 49 (f)

Backward Roll into Straddle Stand *(Fig 50)*

This is altogether much easier to perform and children find it easier to understand. From a normal backward tucked roll the change of shape is made in the pushing stage of the roll so that the skill passes directly from a tuck into a straight leg straddle stand.

Fig 50 Backward roll into straddle stand.

THE SIDE-ROLL *(Fig 51)*

This a complex but basic rolling skill and should be taught using the specific shapes and actions illustrated. The sequence is shown from the start (a) through to the finish (e) but of course the sequence can be performed in reverse order and indeed should be learned in both directions.

Fig 49 (g)

Fig 51 (a)–(e) Side-roll.

Fig 51 (b)

Fig 51 (c)

Fig 51 (d)

Fig 51 (e)

Begin with the kneeling shape (b). Keeping this shape, roll over sideways on to the back at (c) then continue over to (d). The final position is reached by raising the upper body to (e). The start is a mirror image of the finish and so the entire sequence of shapes has now been learned. Note the symmetry of the roll. Note also that if starting with the right leg extended, the roll then moves to the left and finishes with the left leg extended. If starting with the left leg extended, the roll moves to the right and finishes with the right leg extended. Precision of shape is the key to a neat and accurate performance of this skill.

5 Balances

WHAT IS BALANCE?

Balance is a skill. It is the ability to judge exactly where the body is at any time by sensing all those signs which are available to everyone. We all have the same senses – smell, touch, sight, hearing and taste. Of these the senses of smell and taste play little or no role in judging balance. Hearing plays a role in stability, sending information about direction and changing volumes of sound as we move. By sight we can judge distance and also place ourselves in a space. By touch, information on surface pressure and movement can be used to feel changes of contact.

But the body also has a number of internal aids to balance. There are mechanisms, very complex ones, which are comfortable when we are well balanced and uncomfortable when we are not. This 'feeling' is more acute in some people than in others. It in fact acts as a sort of body alarm when it knows that all is not normal, letting us know that a fall is imminent. Then there is also an amazing device in the body which is like an internal sense of touch, feeding information about the muscles and the tendons, the organs and the smallest of fibres back to the brain where a 'spatial picture' is assembled. This picture can identify where an arm is in relation to the foot or where the knee is at a given time. A simple test of this ability is to close the eyes and then place a finger on the tip of the nose. This next exercise can be used to help gymnasts. Sit with a pencil on the table in front of you. Start with both hands on the head. Now close both eyes and pick

Fig 52   Balance. Much of the gymnast's time is spent on the hands and so the gymnast must be able to balance in any situation.

up the pencil. There are many variations on this game which help to develop a sense of spatial awareness.

Note

It is necessary to demonstrate the difference between what is commonly called a balance and the sense of balance which the gymnast uses. A balance is a moment of no movement, a static shape or position. The sense of balance can be used to keep control of the body whilst it is moving. A sense of balance and spatial awareness are both vital skills for the gymnast. With these the gymnast can co-ordinate movements, keep to a rhythm whilst moving and correct position all the time.

LEARNING TO BALANCE

Knowing now what balance is and that everyone has the ability to balance, there is the straightforward task of exercising that ability to improve it.

Stand with the feet apart and follow a simple sequence of arm positions (Fig 53). Now repeat that sequence with the feet together. All the time concentrate on keeping the upper body and the head still. If the balance is failing then stop the arm movement until a recovery is made. Try the sequence with the eyes closed.

The same sequence can be attempted first on one foot then on the other (Fig 54). The slow change of position of the arms will make it easier to adjust for perfect balance. The next stage is to attempt to hold the arms in a fixed position. Like the game of 'statues', at first it is quite tricky but children become skilled in it very quickly.

SCALES AND ARABESQUES

For men and boys one-leg balances are called scales and for girls and women, arabesques. There is no difference in the method of balancing – it is in the shape that the difference lies. For scales the shapes are angular and geometric, while for arabesques the shapes are much softer and follow the balletic curve. The balances illustrated in Figs 55 and 56 are just a few of the many examples to be found. The variations are endless.

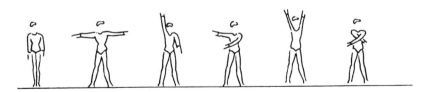

Fig 53   Balance exercise.

Fig 54   Balance exercise.

Balances

Fig 55 (a)–(e) Arabesques 1.

Fig 55 (b)

Fig 55 (c)

Fig 55 (d)

Fig 55 (e)

Fig 56 (a)–(e) Scales 2.

Balances

Fig 56   (b)

Fig 56   (c)

Fig 56 (d)

THE HEADSTAND *(Figs 57–60)*

1. (a)   Begin on the hands and the knees with the hands well forward.

    (b)   Place the head on the floor with the hands and head forming the three points of a triangle.

    (c)   Use the feet to walk fowards until the seat is above the hands.

    (d)   First raise one leg up into a tuck and then use the other foot to check the balance.

    (e)   Carefully raise the other leg into a tuck position.

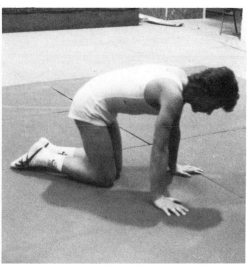

Fig 57   (a)–(e)   Headstand technique.

Fig 56   (e)

Balances

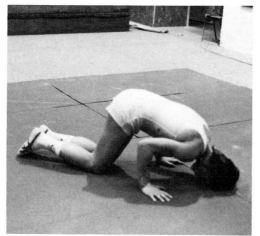

Fig 57 (b)

Fig 57 (c)

Fig 57 (d)

Fig 57 (e)

Fig 59   Headstand variation.

3. Use the corner of a mat to create a triangle as in Fig 60. Place the head in the corner and the hands along the sides of the mat. This will also give the gymnast something to grip to help with balance. Never assume that a young gymnast knows what a triangle shape is.

Fig 58   Headstand variation.

2. The shapes of the headstand can be varied once balance is mastered. The body can be straight (Fig 58), piked (Fig 59), straddled or in splits. There are a variety of combinations to be used.

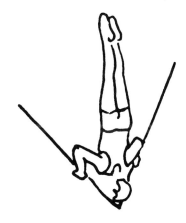

Fig 60   The triangle shape.

Fig 61 (a)–(c) Three versions of the
handstand.

Fig 61 (b)

Fig 61 (c)

THE HANDSTAND (Figs 61–62)

Balancing on the hands is seen to be the greatest skill in children's gymnastics. But like the cart-wheel and the 'roly-poly' there can be great damage done to a handstand by bad practice and misconceptions. Firstly, look at the three contrasting handstands shown in Fig 61. Only one is correct.

In (a) the feet overhang the support and balance is maintained by pushing the shoulders back towards a bridge position. In this shape the gymnast often falls over with no correction possible. In handstand (b) the shoulders are in front of the support with the back hollow and the head up. With this handstand it is possible to stay in balance by walking. Handstand (c) is correctly shaped. The weight of all the major parts of the body pass directly through the support. The shape is slim and straight with the ankles extended and the head held in line with the

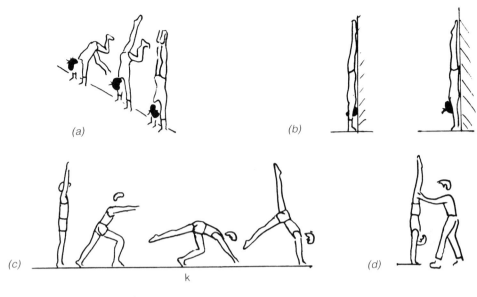

(e)

Fig 62 (a)–(e) Handstand technique.

spine. The seat is tight to keep the body in tension. The balance is adjusted by pressing on the fingers and making small movements of the shoulders.

Balance the correct shape up against the wall (*see* Fig 62 (a)). Facing into the wall and facing out will make the gymnast adopt the right shape and will build up an awareness of balance and strength (*see* Fig 62 (b)). To start with, stay in balance for only a few seconds but each time stay longer until one full minute can be held.

When kicking to handstand (*see* Fig 62 (c)) step well forward and reach along the floor to create a strong key position (k). The swing of the rear leg and the push from the bent leg work together. Supporters should catch between the knee and the thigh, never by the feet or the clothing. The supporter taps the gymnast into balance with light contact.

6 Agilities

THE CART-WHEEL
(Figs 64–65)

The cart-wheel is perhaps the first activity which a young gymnast will associate with those events viewed on television at Olympic games and world championships. It is the first agility to be learned and is often seen as a playground challenge. The cart-wheel for gymnastics, however, must be very precise.

1.   (a)   From a standing position, raise the arms and then, raising one leg, make a quarter-turn.
  (b)   Leaning well over, take a large step to the side and reach with both arms over the head for the floor. One side of the body will be fully stretched whilst the leading leg bends to bring the hand into contact with the floor.
  (c)   When the leading hand reaches the floor the trailing leg swings quickly overhead with the bent leg pushing to increase the movement into the cart-wheel.
  (d)   Passing sideways through the handstand the legs should be as wide as possible. A straight-line box splits is perfect.
  (e)   The final part of the cart-wheel, the recovery, should be a mirror image in shape to the first part with one side fully stretched. The recovery leg bends to absorb the motion then pushes the body upright once more. The cart-wheel ends in a sideways position.
2.   Try to find situations in which the

Fig 63   *Agility. Modern skills can be complex. The body must be quick to learn new patterns of movement.*

Fig 64 (a)–(e) Cart-wheel technique.

Fig 65 (a)–(c) Cart-wheel progressions.

gymnast can find out how to co-ordinate the leg-swing and push with the transfer of weight from one hand to the other. In the situation shown in Fig 65 (a), the child will be able to try passing from one side of the line to the other in either direction.

3. A circle is easier to follow when learning the cart-wheel than a straight line (Fig 65 (b)). The smaller the circle, the easier the cart-wheel will be to perform.

4. The use of a slope can assist the gymnast in maintaining the energy in the cart-wheel (*see* Fig 65 (c)).

THE HEADSPRING (Figs 66–68)

The headspring is most commonly seen performed by boys, but in the past few years it has been used extensively by girls as a linking element in floor exercises to combine two series of agilities.

1. (a) From a standing position, raise the arms forwards.
(b) As the gymnast begins to fall forwards off-balance, the knees bend forwards and down.

Agilities

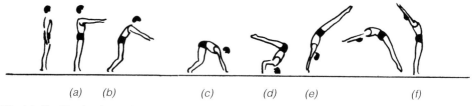

(a)   (b)   (c)   (d)   (e)   (f)

Fig 66   (a)–(f)   Headspring technique.

(c)   When the hands reach the floor the legs are still bent, coiled like a spring ready to drive the headspring over.

(d)   Straighten the legs so that the gymnast is pushed through a piked headstand position. Note that this is not a held headstand. To begin with, the hands and the head make a strong and stable triangular base which we would expect in the headstand, but at a more advanced level the hands and head create a straight line which makes for a more powerful pushing position.

(e)   Release the pike to make an arched shape and then push with the arms into flight.

(f)   The arms remain above the head. The flight stage is completed by straightening the back to stand upright.

2.   Headspring from a box (Fig 67). From a static held position, which can be corrected if wrong, the gymnast makes a maximum effort to extend, to swing the legs over and to push the arms straight. The coach, or coaches, can guide the action upwards to allow the gymnast to sense the thrust from the box top. The coach then places the gymnast back on the box in a handstand without the gymnast completing the headspring. Use a box so that the seat passes over the hands by sliding along the box top. When the feet reach the end of the box the headspring is performed.

3.   From an extended jump, make a headspring over a low box or pile of mats (Fig 68). Lower the platform as the headspring improves.

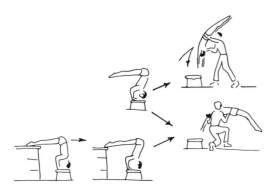

Fig 67   Headspring progressions.

Fig 68   Headspring progression.

THE NECKSPRING (Figs 69–70)

The neckspring is a much slower element than the headspring and requires great suppleness in the shoulders and the back. Such a slow element is now unpopular but the neckspring does appear in set exercises.

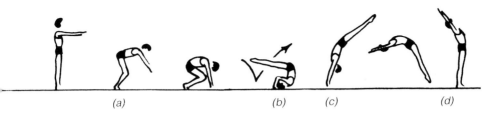

69 (a)–(d) Neckspring technique.

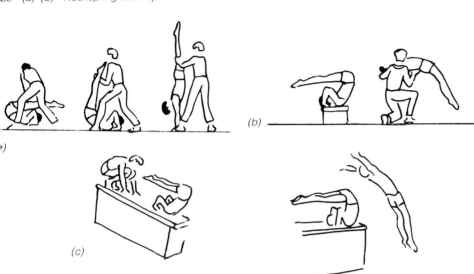

70 (a)–(c) Neckspring progressions.

(a)   From a standing position bend the legs to a crouch and place the hands on the floor about one arm's length away from the feet. The neckspring has a slow and exact entry and you must not attempt to push it along the floor or build up forward speed.

(b)   The arms bend and the back of the head and the top of the shoulders are placed on the floor. The straightened legs then fold down towards the floor making a bouncing action which then combines with . . .

(c)   . . . a rapid arm extension and swing of the legs overhead.

(d)   The neckspring requires a significant hollow in the back if it is to be raised to a stand (compare with the arch in the headspring). As the gymnast becomes upright the back straightens and the arms remain held up.

2.   The position from which the push is made is very cramped and the gymnast will gain experience of this by pushing up to the handstand from the shoulders (Fig 70 (a)).

3.   In view of the high levels of strength and suppleness required for the neckspring, the gymnast must be prepared to spend some time working from a box top or a stack of mats until there is a good chance of completing the skill successfully (Fig 70 (b–c)).

(a)   From a held position on a box top, the push is assisted through a hollow flight shape to a stand.

(b)   Progress by reducing the height of the platform. Start from a crouch and slowly roll into position before pushing into flight.

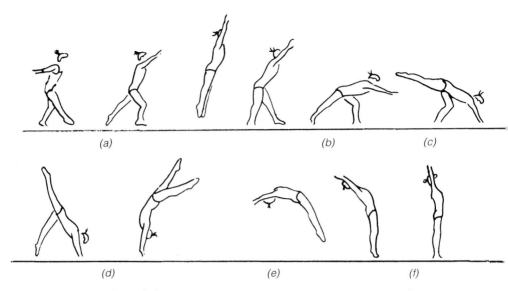

Fig 71 (a)–(f) Handspring technique.

THE HANDSPRING

(Figs 71–72)

The handspring is one of the most complex and difficult skills to perform correctly. It is also the most badly performed at school and club level with many faults never being put right. The sensation of leaping over hands on to feet can be a tremendous motivation but can also lead to complacency and bad technique when the lessons of basic shaping are forgotten.

1. (a) The handspring comes from a forward-leaning stretch jump where the arms are held high. The arms swing upwards and forwards to carry the gymnast along the floor as well as up.
(b) As the jump lands the weight is pushed forward on to one leg. The step forward is a long one with the leading leg bending to bring the upper body down and also to prepare like a spring ready to push. The shoulders and the arms swing down together with the head looking at the hands all the time.

(c) This is a key position. Note that the shoulders are well down and the hands are well forward. Also, the head is up, the back leg is in a position to swing overhead and the lower leg is bent as it prepares to push the body up and over. The rotation for the handspring is mostly provided by the run, the swinging back leg and the bent leg as it straightens. The lift is mostly provided by the shoulders with a sharp extension through a handstand position. The head must be allowed to fall back a little and should be held back until the handspring is upright.
(d) All the driving mechanisms are in operation together. Swing the back leg over, push the bent leg straight and extend rapidly out of the shoulders.
(e) In flight the body is held in an arched shape and the feet are brought together. The arms remain aloft and the head is back a little.
(f) On landing the seat is tightened and the back straightened, and finally the head is returned to its natural alignment.

Fig 72 (a)–(e) Handspring progressions.

2. One of the major problems with the handspring is finding the key position (Fig 72 (a)). Practise from a stand with the arms raised then step and reach into a held key position. If the gymnast adds to this a strong push from the shoulders he or she will jump into a handstand (Fig 72 (b)). This is a difficult but invaluable practice.

3. For this practice the services of a coach are necessary (Fig 72 (c)). The flight shape is added to the previous stage by allowing the coach to guide the gymnast from hand-stand upwards before returning to the handstand. An experienced coach will be able to help correct the shape.

4. The coach can now support the gymnast through the completed handspring (Fig 72 (d)). From a standing start make a stretch jump and reach into the handspring with the coach lifting the gymnast to stand upright once again. The head should be allowed to stay back until the floor is reached.

5. Where classes are learning a hand-spring the coach will find it much easier to support with gymnasts performing off a box (Fig 72 (e)). A gentle slope makes the hand-spring easier. The coach supports the gymnast all the way to the floor mat, until a still standing position is reached.

Fig 73 (a)–(g) Flic-flac technique.

THE FLIC-FLAC *(Figs 73–75)*

The flic-flac is also known as the back flip, the flip-flop and from the distant past, the lion's leap. The flic-flac is the major skill used to gain speed when moving backwards. It is an accelerator used to build up energy to be transferred for instance into a somersault. Its role is therefore a vital one in advanced gymnastics. It is also perhaps the first element of risk which will confront the newcomer to gymnastics. Landing on the head or the back must be avoided and so the flic-flac should only be attempted whilst under supervision and assistance from an experienced and qualified coach.

1. (a) Begin from a standing position, raising the arms above the head, keeping the seat tight and the head held still.
   (b) Leaning back to be off balance, draw the seat downwards and backwards as if you are sitting in an invisible chair. The arms reach down and backwards, the head remains still. The spring mechanism of the element is now set to release its energy. Note how far back the seat and the shoulders are in relation to the feet which are still in their original position.
   (c) Swing the arms upwards and backwards, reaching over the head. The head then follows the arms, with the gymnast watching the hands.

(d) With the arms well into their swing stage the legs can extend pushing the upper body into the flic-flac. This is a pushing action with the feet flat on the floor and the legs fully extended and straight.
(e) The arms swing and the shoulders lead the body into a hollow position, looking for the floor and an early hand contact. The support position is reached well before the lower body passes over the hands.
(f) Sometimes called the snapper action. This is a rapid change from a hollow back to a dished-back shape. This requires great strength and control to perform accurately. It is very much the essence of a good flic-flac. This snapping round of the back permits a powerful push through the shoulders which drives the body upright and on to the feet.

Fig 74 Incorrect landing positions for the flic-flac.

(g) The landing position is upright with the arms raised. Any pike or hollow recovery from the flic-flac, as shown in Fig 74, will be quite wrong and will make it impossible to use the flic-flac for combining agilities.

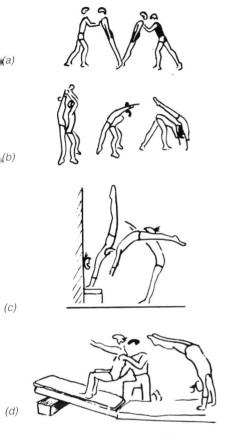

Fig 75 (a)–(d) Flic-flac progressions.

this exercise. From a small arch, begin to fall from a handstand before sharply pushing and rounding the spine. It will take a great deal of time and effort to learn how to go from this exercise into an upright position.

5. Finally, progressive reducing of assistance with shaping and lifting will allow the gymnast to learn the correct technique. Often the flic-flac is attempted before the gymnast is capable of making the best action possible. In such a case the skill will *never* be powerful and may in fact end with injury.

THE ARAB-SPRING
(Figs 76–77)

The arab-spring is also at times known as the round-off or the cart-wheel with quarter-turn. The latter reveals the problem which this skill has inherited. Very often it is taught as an afterthought, just by putting a quarter-turn on the end of the cart-wheel. Yet the arab-spring has a technique of its own and must be learned as a new skill without reference to other movements. Furthermore, the element must not be used to link into a back flip until it has been perfected.

The complex setting of the body spring and the changing back shapes make the arab-spring a very difficult skill to perform. It is very easy to perform with total disregard for technique. It must be emphasised that the arab-spring poorly performed will be a positive disadvantage in learning combined agilities.

2. To help understand the off-balance opening for the back flip, gymnasts can help each other with this exercise. A rigid and straight body leans first backwards then forwards to be caught at about 10 degrees past the vertical.

3. This time the partner holds the arms just above the shoulder and lifts from under the seat to carry the gymnast over into an arched shape which can be lowered into a handstand. This is not suitable for very young children because they do not work well in pairs or understand the hazards of falling backwards.

4. The snapper action can be isolated with

1. (a) The arab-spring is produced from a run and is preceded by a stretch jump with the arms raised upwards and forwards. The body leans forward. The jump must not be performed with a hollow in the small of the back.

Agilities

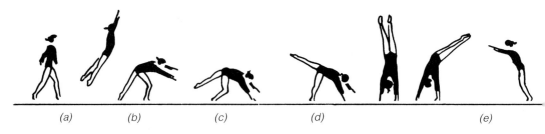

(a)	(b)	(c)	(d)	(e)

Fig 76   (a)–(e)   Arab-spring technique.

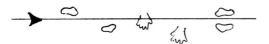

Fig 76   (f)   The placement of the hands for the arab-spring.

(b)   The leading leg slides forwards close to the floor as the upper body folds down to reach ahead of the feet. The placement of the hands has been the source of great discussion and some change over the years. The traditional straight-line pattern has been generally replaced now by the one shown in Fig 76 (f). Consider that at stage (b) the shoulders begin by folding down towards the floor still facing forwards. They begin to turn by 90 degrees, a quarter-turn, as the hands approach the floor. In the case illustrated in Fig 76 (f) the right leg is leading and the right hand is placed on the centre line. The second hand should be placed further to the right of the centre line, facing backwards. As the body swings over the hands this will make pushing in the last stages of the arab-spring much more efficient and less awkward.

(c)   The leading hand arrives on the floor with the leading leg bending. Once again we see that a powerful spring has been set.

(d)   The bent leg now pushes and the rear leg swings overhead giving great energy and rotation to the element.

(e)   The lift is provided by a strong push from the shoulders. A first quarter-turn is produced during the hand placement and a second quarter-turn is made through the pushing stage from the hands to the feet. The back snaps into a dished shape with the feet pulling down and the shoulders rising rapidly to complete the arab-spring, finishing upright with the arms raised overhead.

2.   From kneeling on a bench (Fig 77 (a)), raise the arms overhead. Step off the bench with one leg and with the shoulders still facing the floor fold down on to the leading leg. Turn the shoulders just before the hands touch the floor and then cart-wheel away from the bench.

3.   Use a bench and a springboard for this progression shown in Fig 77 (b). The leading leg once more steps upwards and forwards and the chest folds down, making a late turn into a cart-wheel. Complete the second quarter-turn during the pushing stage. The feet snap down to drive the gymnast upright and backwards into a raised safety mat against a wall. This requires careful measurements to be accurate.

4.   Use a small stack of mats as a platform to arab-spring across (Fig 77 (c)). As the skill improves less mats can be used. This will assist in bringing the gymnast upright.

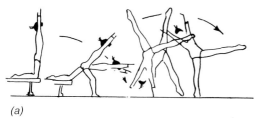

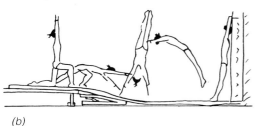

Fig 77 (a)–(c) Arab-spring progressions.

DIVE FORWARD ROLL
(Figs 78–79)

The dive forward roll is perhaps the most spectacular of the simple skills but it requires technical accuracy to perform safely. Using a two-footed jump it can be given great height, but attention must be given to the hazards of landing and rolling. Use mats that will absorb the momentum from the dive on landing.

1. (a) The run and the jump involve the same hurdle step as in vaulting. Draw the arms back and bring the feet together before making the jump. Whilst making the jump swing the arms forwards and upwards, punching out and up into the air.

   (b) The flight shape is a gentle hollow. The heels and the legs lift to the rear. They must be higher than the chest and the arms at the top of the dive in order to make a safe landing. A horizontal or feet

Fig 78 (a)–(c) Dive forward roll technique.

Agilities

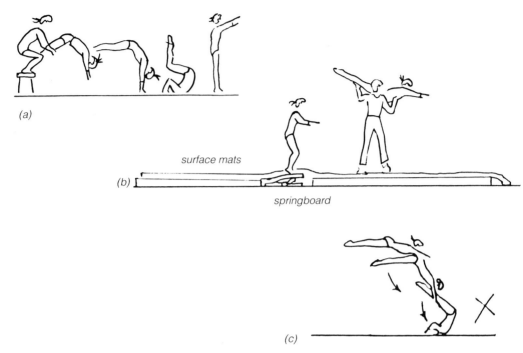

(a)

surface mats

(b)

springboard

(c)

Fig 79 (a)–(c) Dive forward roll progressions.

lower than shoulders position is extremely hazardous. A coach must always assist with this element to correct any fault in flight until absolutely safe.

(c) The recovery and roll to a stand will present few problems if the correct flight position has been found. With the heels and the legs still held high, reach down with the arms and the shoulders for the floor. As the hands make contact with the mats tuck the head under and carry the weight first on the bending arms and then on the shoulders as the roll begins. Swing the arms forwards and upwards to assist with the recovery.

2. Build up confidence in the landing and recovery stage by rolling from a box top (Fig 79 (a)).

3. Use a matted runway with a springboard to make the jump easier (Fig 79 (b)). A coach will be able to assist with the flight shape and ensure safety.

4. Lifting the chest at the expense of the legs will place a great deal of stress on the back and the shoulders during the roll (Fig 79 (c)).

A BOY'S FLOOR EXERCISE
(Fig 80)

The essence of a boy's floor exercise is a continuous and harmonious combination of elements. The exercise should include high movements such as jumps, low movements such as rolls, a handstand element, a balance and some agilities. The style should not be overtly balletic with soft arm movements but should produce a clean and crisp effect with the head and the arms used as part of the linking forms.

Fig 80   A boy's floor exercise.

1.   From a stand, cart-wheel to stand.
2.   Making a quarter-turn, step forward to make a scissor jump.
3.   Step forward, kicking through a handstand and a forward roll to stand.
4.   Step forward and single leg balance.
5.   Stretch jump with a half-turn.
6.   From a short run, arab-spring and stretch jump.

Fig 81   Grace. Most top gymnasts are expert dancers.

A GIRL'S FLOOR EXERCISE
(Fig 82)

Select a short piece of music to suit the gymnast. Avoid well-known tunes, especially those with a popular lyric, and powerfully orchestrated pieces which are difficult to work to. Instead choose something light and rhythmic, using for example just a piano. The opening must be bold and strong. Unless the gymnast has great ability as a dancer, do not use slow or waltz-time music.

Study the key positions and shapes marked k in Fig 82. The gymnast should learn to move in and out of these for effect. The arms should be kept soft, and use turns of the head for dramatic effect. Look for a slow passage of dance steps and a rapid contrast into the agilities.

Fig 82   A girl's floor exercise.

1. Dance a series of steps and adopt set poses or positions.
2. Make a quarter-turn into a cart-wheel and a quarter-turn out.
3. Move in to a short run and a handspring.

4. A leap with a turn followed by movements at floor level.
5. From a short run perform a split-leap and turn into a finish.

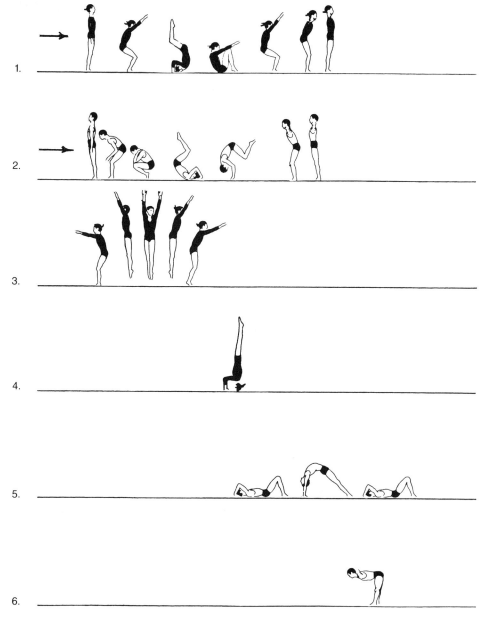

Fig 83   Floor level 1.

FLOOR SKILLS

Level 1 *(Fig 83)*

1. Forward roll.
2. Backward roll.
3. Jump with a half-turn.
4. Headstand.
5. Bridge.
6. Straddle stand.

Fig 84   Floor level 2.

Level 2 *(Fig 84)*

1. Kick to handstand.
2. Cart-wheel.
3. Splits.
4. From stand, high forward roll.
5. Handstand forward roll.
6. Backward roll to straddle stand.

Agilities

Fig 85   Floor level 3.

Level 3 (Fig 85)

1. From bridge kick through handstand.
2. Three different jumps.
3. One-arm cart-wheel.
4. Backward roll through handstand.
5. Dive forward roll from a run.
6. From straddle sit, lower chest to floor.

Fig 86   Floor level 4.

Level 4 *(Fig 86)*

1. From handstand, drop to bridge.
2. Dive cart-wheel.
3. From stand, fall to front support.
4. Held V-sit.
5. Arab-spring (round-off).
6. Jump with a full turn.

Agilities

Fig 87   Floor level 5.

Level 5 *(Fig 87)*

1. Forward walk-over.
2. Handspring.
3. Split-leap.
4. Piked backward roll through handstand.
5. Three different cart-wheels.
6. A shaped handstand, stag or split.

Fig 88 Floor level 6.

Level 6 *(Fig 88)*

1. Backward walk-over.
2. Flic-flac (back flip).
3. Three consecutive cart-wheels.

4. Lift to handstand from straddle strand.
5. Two different splits.
6. Handspring to dive forward roll.

7 Vaulting

Vaulting takes its inspiration from the natural instinct to leap over obstacles. Whether as a test of strength or of courage, or simply as an easy way of getting from A to B, vaulting has been performed for many centuries. In the Mediterranean the ancients leapt over charging bulls and in the Middle Ages vaulting was a practice for horsemanship. However, in modern times vaulters have

Fig 89 *Courage. Through skill and confidence the gymnast will develop the courage to include gravity-defying movements in their exercise.*

been careful to select an immovable obstacle, sometimes called a box or, if it has legs, a horse.

At its simplest, vaulting can be like the straightforward game of leap-frog which is played all over the world. From a run a two-footed jump is made, and with assistance from the arms one child can leap over another. At its most advanced, vaulting introduces an element of somersaulting which can be very spectacular.

Simple vaulting uses a beat board (a small sprung ramp) or a springboard (a padded wooden spring). The beat board is still found in schools but is now mostly replaced with a modern springboard. Experienced gymnasts may also use a trampette (a small trampoline). But trampettes must never be used unless under the direct supervision of a qualified and experienced coach. Like many other pieces of equipment, when used wrongly the trampette can cause serious accidents. Beat boards and springboards are similar to popguns to propel gymnasts; trampettes are like powerful cannons to be treated with care and respect.

THE LEAP-FROG *(Figs 90–91)*

Within cities, climbing and scrambling around has been sadly declining as a children's pastime. Playground games have changed over the past decade and have been replaced by more individual indoor activities. But the simple leap-frog has survived all changes and may still be seen

this leads to ⟶   this leads to ⟶

Fig 90   Leap-frog technique.

every day in any recreation area. Children learn this skill by watching each other, by trial and error and by enjoying the fun of the chase or competition.

The leap-frog is a useful vaulting progression and can be a valid warm-up activity. It can be adapted to be used in many games to motivate children to run around and become warm. However, very young children (say under-nines) find the situation of being the human box difficult and so they must be taught how to remain firm for the 'frog' to leap over.

(a)   Each team is evenly spaced (see Fig 91). Starting with the child at the back, the entire team must be vaulted. Once at the front, the child races to the rear then taps the next child on the shoulder as a sign for him to begin. Each child must vault every team member so that after racing from front to back he must vault down the line to his place before giving the signal to the next child.

(b)   Here the game is to leap-frog one child and crawl through the legs of the next. Over and under is always the order.

(c)   A little more complicated: over the first child then around and under the next.

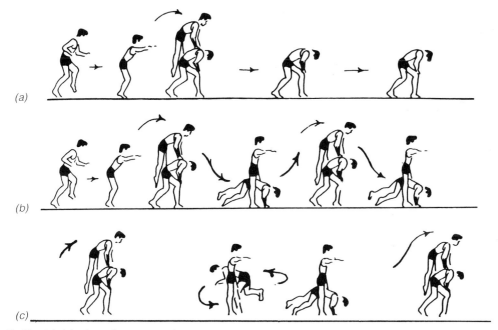

(a)

(b)

(c)

Fig 91   (a)–(c)   Leap-frog progressions.

THE SEVEN STAGES OF VAULTING *(Figs 92–97)*

1. The Run (Fig 92) The run-up must be fast and well balanced. Rapid acceleration will be made when the thrusting leg picks up with the knees high. Run with the palms turned a little upwards. Do not cross the arms as this will cause the hips and shoulders to roll.

Fig 92   The run-up.

2. The Hurdle Step (Fig 93) This is the method of changing from a run into a two-footed jump. Start from a standing position. Hold the arms back. From one step forward, hop to land on both feet. The arms remain held back. Try hopscotch!

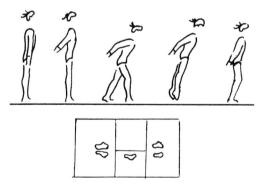

Fig 93   The hurdle step.

3. The Jump (Fig 94) The jump is made with the upper body upright. The arms swing upwards and forwards and the jump is made from a short bend of the legs. The seat is tightened and the legs extended. Practise repetition jumps on a springboard before making a simple stretch jump. Height can be gained by jumping over a box top. Ensure at this stage that the arms are working correctly.

Fig 94   The jump.

4. (and 6.) Flight (Fig 95) There are two flight stages to vaulting. The first follows the jump most often with a straight body shape, and the second comes after the push from the box. The second flight shape

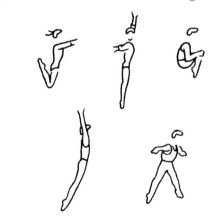

Fig 95   The flight stages.

often describes the vault performed, for example the vertical straddle vault. If we return to Chapter 3 on shapes we can see most of the vault positions and just how they are constructed. Practise jumping from a box top making different flight shapes.

5. The Thrust (Fig 96) The thrust or pushing stage from the box creates height for the second flight. It requires strength in the shoulders and back and a dynamic extension through the arms. Look once more at Chapter 2 which covered conditioning and strength work for the arms and the shoulders.

Fig 97   Landing.

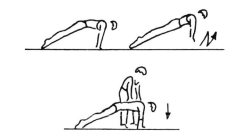

Fig 96   The thrust.

6.   Flight   (*see* 4.)

7.   Landing   (Fig 97) Even though this is the seventh stage and the final part of the vault, it is usual to teach the landing technique to start with. Never enter a situation blind! The landing absorbs all the force from the run and the flight, and the legs and ankles must be educated to cope with this strenuous task. Practise landings from a low box top. Step off the box and then lift the arms forward and open (for balance). Land on the flat of the feet (not on the toes), making a short bend of the legs to absorb the force but keeping the upper body upright. The feet should be slightly open and the knees and the feet turned out a little. This is a very similar technique to the dancer's half-plié.

THE SIMPLE VAULT *(Fig 98)*

Drilling a class in the very repetitive process of learning the technique of simple vaulting can be laborious. A simple arrangement of apparatus can create a training situation which is to some extent self-correcting. The following exercise assists with all but stage 5, the thrust stage. The apparatus required will be a landing mat, a springboard, a box top and a short runway of mats (or a bench).

Start from a standing position and take the arms back. Use one foot to step over the box top and, bringing both feet together, rebound from the springboard, making a stretch jump to a still landing. On landing, hold still with the legs bent until balance is reached before standing upright. With the feet and the knees turned out a little and with the legs bending a very stable landing shape is created. Do not land standing upright with the legs straight. Absorb the energy with the legs, recover the balance, then stand up straight.

To vary the exercise, use the same situation from a walk in at the start, then use different jump shapes for variety and for competitions. Later the box top can be removed as the hurdle step improves.

Vaulting

(a)

(b)

Fig 98   (a) and (b)   Simple vaulting exercises.

THE VERTICAL VAULTS
(Fig 99)

The most straightforward of the vaults are those which require the gymnast to remain upright. We have already examined the role of the leap-frog vault. With a basic grounding of the techniques involved in the seven stages of vaulting, the gymnast is then armed with the skills to attempt the vertical vaults. Of these the first to be taught is the jump-on to jump-off vault. This is not strictly speaking a vault at all as the feet touch the horse, but it is a sound progression for co-ordination and is the easiest way in which to introduce young gymnasts to the apparatus.

Start with a low box and a springboard. Place both hands on the box and simply rebound up and down on the board. The next progression will be to lift the seat and pass the shoulders forward until the feet reach the top of the box. Many children will need to use their knees at first. This is a step towards building confidence. Encourage the child to place the feet on the box and eventually they will, even if it takes many attempts. The coach can support by holding the shoulder with one hand and lifting lightly under the seat with the other. For the first few attempts place the box lengthways. A fall from the box or even seeing a short vertical drop on the other side of the box can inhibit learning. Finish the exercise with a stretch jump to a safe and still landing. Reinforce landing technique!

Fig 99   Vertical vault technique.

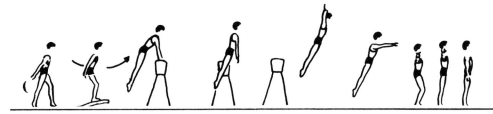

Fig 100   Vertical astride vault technique.

Vertical Astride Vault *(Fig 100)*

The closest vault to the leap-frog is the vertical astride vault. This is performed on a buck which allows the legs to remain under the gymnast as the straddle is made passing either side of the apparatus.

From the jump reach forward with the hands and push down. Lift the chest and hold up the head. Notice that there is a very short flight stage before the push from the buck. This is the first flight stage and should show a small pike. The second flight stage from the push to the landing is straight with the chest showing and the arms forward and open. The straddle or astride position is achieved only when the hands strike the buck.

It is wrong to straddle immediately after the jump, since the first flight should be performed with the feet together. The most difficult aspect for the gymnast is always the arm positions. From the push off the buck the arms lift up with the second flight and then pass forward and open for the landing stage.

Support for the vertical astride vault requires experience and lightness of foot (Fig 101). The coach stands facing the gymnast and reaches for the upper arms. As the push stage and the second flight begin the coach steps back carrying the gymnast off the buck. Clearly the landing mats must

Fig 101   Supporting the vertical astride vault.

be firm and free of obstruction. The coach will be required in the early attempts when the gymnast only takes a few running steps.

Tucked-Through Vault *(Fig 102)*

The tucked-through vault presents the young gymnast with the more demanding task of squatting the feet between the hands. Whilst this can be seen to be a logical progression from the jump-on jump-off vault it is surprisingly a much more complex problem than the vertical astride vault. As well as pushing high into second flight the gymnast must be able to first lift the seat to make the space through which the legs may pass. The vault is best learned with the assistance of a coach who stands at the side of the apparatus. Once again the buck is of great use as it puts the coach in a position closer to the gymnast. If a buck is not available then vault to one side of a box placed crossways. The coach holds the upper arm with one hand and lifts under the seat with the other. It is relatively easy to

Fig 102   Tucked-through vault technique.

assist this vault and often confidence alone is the key to success.

A much more effective thrust stage is now required to clear the box and the gymnast will need to continue to exercise for strength in the shoulders and the arms. After the lift off the box the second flight stage will be completed by a full extension of the body before landing. Weak vaults will have poor flight shapes and it must be emphasised that it is the shape which defines the vault. A tucked shape means that the back is round, the knees are drawn up and the ankles are extended. Since the second flight stage of this vault has two contrasting shapes in it the transition must be instant for effect. Do not blend the shapes in the second flight so that they become half-tucked and half-straight.

THE HORIZONTAL VAULTS
(Fig 103)

In this group of vaults the first flight stage reaches up and backwards to, or just past, a horizontal line through the shoulders. With the body-weight in this horizontal position the thrust is much more efficient and powerful giving greater second flight. These are vaults of counter-rotation. This is a grand name to describe how in the first flight the legs are swinging up and backwards, and in the second flight they are swinging down and forwards. The first flight shows a forward somersault rotation and the second flight shows a backward somersault rotation.

For this type of vault the gymnast must increase the run-up to gain speed. A long but slow run-up is of little use. Speed produces the force which lifts the gymnast. It is possible to learn to raise the body in the first flight and to use a strong thrust to gain counter-rotation at the same time.

Use a springboard, a horse placed cross-ways (a buck or cross-box will do), and a stack of safety mats with a firm surface. By making adjustments the gymnast can learn to lift the legs to the rear and find the new thrust position. On striking the horse, change the back shape from arched to dished. Land in either an open tuck or in a dished astride position. The hands and the feet should land on the surface of the mats at the same time to demonstrate that counter-rotation has been achieved (*see* Fig 103 (a)). Once this has been mastered then the progression into second flight without the mats can be made. The upper body is lifted during the second flight to find an upright landing (*see* Fig 103 (b)).

If the first flight is below horizontal then less lift is created and often if the first flight is neither horizontal nor vertical then both the thrust stage and the second flight stage fail to develop. The necessity to over-pike in the second flight stage often results from an ill-defined angle when the hands reach the horse. The feet are travelling too quickly for a vertical astride vault and there is insufficent

Fig 103 (a)–(d) Horizontal vault technique.

lift. As a result the feet must come through sharply with a pike to ensure a safe landing (*see* Fig 103 (c)).

The straight leg squat is made with a very sharp pike and then a stretch in the second flight. This vault requires great strength and suppleness (*see* Fig 103 (d)). Note the full extension before landing and how far back the shoulders must be in the first flight, so the gymnast has time to make the correct shapes.

THE OVERSWING VAULTS

All of the major vaults used by competitive gymnasts involve complete rotations of the body and a somersault from the feet to land on the feet with an assisting push or a thrust from the hands off the horse. There are three vaults in this category for the young gymnast

to learn and they provide the basis for every known vault.

The Handspring *(Fig 104)*

The handspring is sometimes called the overswing or the long arm overswing. In shape it is relatively simple to understand since the gymnast remains arched during most of the vault. It relies upon the gymnast making a run-up with enough speed to maintain a long shape during rotation. Needless to say both the run and the jump must be well performed.

In the first flight reach up and forwards with the arms towards the horse. Keep the head up. Raise the legs until they are between 10 and 5 minutes to the hour like the rotation on a clock face. At that point the hands make contact with the horse and the thrust stage begins. During the thrust keep the head still.

Vaulting

Fig 104   Handspring vault technique.

Tighten the seat to pull the legs over the top of the vault and into the second flight. The arch shape is maintained in the second flight with the head falling back a little to assist with shaping.

There is a school of thought which prefers to make the thrust stage and the second flight very straight, but I believe that allowing a natural arch in the upper back during the second flight and letting the head drop back a fraction improves the rotation. The landing and the recovery are made with the head drawing forwards and as always with the arms opening out and the legs absorbing the remaining movement.

Common Faults

There is no question that the handspring is the most badly performed vault, partly because it is the most common, partly because it is at the top end of the basic ability range, but mostly because many gymnasts try to make the vault before they have made the appropriate progressions in the learning process. The most common faults are caused by attempting to handspring on too high a horse too early. Often the height of the horse is set at the minimum competition height. That is invariably too high to learn on. The key to understanding the learning process lies in appreciating that

the horse can only be high enough to accommodate the speed of the run and the technique mastered at that time. Do not be in a hurry. Better a well-shaped and well-directed vault on a box a metre high than a misshapen failure at just over a metre.

Use a sectional box to advantage, or try a small box placed lengthways to encourage reach during the first flight stage. Alternatively, use two springboards to assist with the jump, and get a coach to shape and direct the vault (*see* Fig 105).

(a)   From a short run-up, jump to a handstand on a low box top. A coach can assist

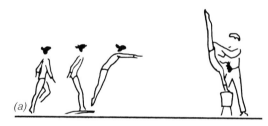

(a)

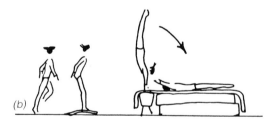

(b)

(c)

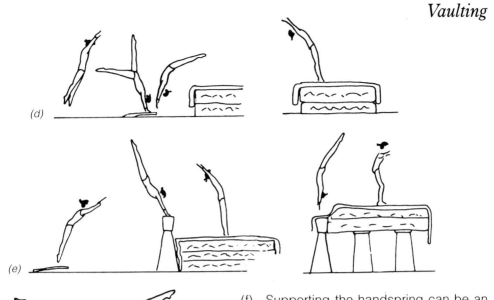

'Fig 105 (a)–(f) Handspring vault progressions.

(f) Supporting the handspring can be an advantage from either side of the horse. If shaping the first flight, stand between the board and the horse. If assisting the second flight, stand at the landing area. Never throw the heels without checking that the chest and shoulders are correctly placed.

The Cart-Wheel *(Fig 106)*

by holding the handstand. Note that this is not a hands-on and push-to-handstand – the gymnast is trying to land in a handstand. Progress to a higher box and use a padded wall.

(b) From a short run-up jump to a handstand before dropping with the back flat on to some safety mats. Note that it is not enough to roll down – the gymnast must show a handstand.

(c) From standing on a horse placed lengthways, handspring off to a stand.

(d) Use a springboard to make a handspring to stand, then raise the landing mat height to promote lift in the second flight stage.

(e) Make an overswing vault, landing on a high surface. This can be extended to a height well above the level of the horse.

For boys the cart-wheel on the long horse is a vault in its own right. For girls it is a progression towards more complex vaults on the cross-horse. The cart-wheel will be the first time that a twist is introduced to the vault class.

The quarter-turn appears in the first flight. The run, hurdle step and jump are as before, but early in the first flight as the gymnast is reaching for the horse the shoulders turn. The top arm (in Fig 106 the left arm) reaches to the end of the horse and will serve to thrust in the usual way to gain lift. The lower arm (in Fig 106 the right arm) reaches for the centre of the horse. With a lower position of the body at the moment of thrust, it bends to find a good position from which to push and add to the rotation. The lower bent arm acts in the same way as the bent leading leg in the first

79

Vaulting

Fig 106   Cart-wheel vault technique.

half of the handspring. The feet remain together throughout the vault, and the gymnast remains sideways to the line of the run-up. The landing is a little more awkward with the feet apart to make a stable base to collect the balance before standing up.

The Arab-Spring (Figs 107–108)

The arab-spring vault can be treated as a cart-wheel with a quarter-turn at the end to face the horse. Once again it is a preparatory vault for other more advanced movements and should be included in the gymnast's repertoire. For boys the cart-wheel remains exactly as before with a quarter-turn on to the horse and a quarter-turn off. In the second flight stage the body

shape is dished with an emphasis on an early upright position well before landing.

For girls there will be rather more than a quarter-turn in the first flight. The narrow top of the cross-horse will not allow the arms to spread wide apart. Therefore the body rises closer to the vertical as the hands thrust, leaving very little of the turn to complete for the change of direction. The emphasis in the second flight stage is once more on a dished body shape and an early upright position. Landing facing the horse is much easier than landing facing away from it.

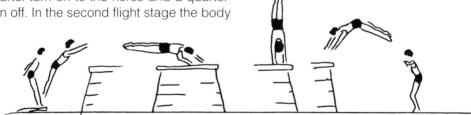

Fig 107   The arab-spring vault for boys.

Fig 108   The arab-spring vault for girls.

80

Fig 109   Vault level 1.

VAULT SKILLS

Level 1 *(Fig 109)*

1.   Stretch jump.
2.   Stretch jump from a bench.
3.   Run and stretch jump.
4.   Run and stretch jump from a spring-board.
5.   Run and tuck jump from a springboard.
6.   Stretch jump from a springboard to land on a bench.

Vaulting

Fig 110   Vault level 2.

Level 2 *(Fig 110)*

1. Squat on and stretch jump off.
2. 10 metre (11 yard) sprint.
3. Stretch jump over a bench.
4. Sargent jump (measured height).
5. Vault to straddle stand.
6. Jump from a springboard with heels by the seat.

Fig 111   Vault level 3.

Level 3 *(Fig 111)*

1.   Squat on and tuck jump off.
2.   Vertical astride vault.
3.   Jump with half-turn.

4.   Star jump with hand-clap.
5.   Front support, hollow, push to stand.
6.   3 rebound jumps on the springboard.

Vaulting

Fig 112   Vault level 4.

Level 4 *(Fig 112)*

1. Tucked through vault.
2. Jump on and jump off with a half-turn.
3. Squat on with a rolled-up mat (or padded obstacle) between the board and the horse.
4. From a stand on the long horse, arabspring off to stand.
5. Using two springboards end to end, from stand on the first board jump to the second board and squat on to the horse.
6. From a stand place one leg forward, swing the arms from behind and jump into a handstand.

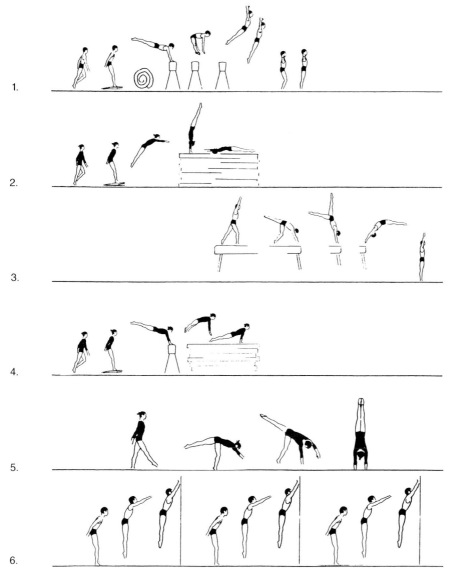

Fig 113   Vault level 5.

Level 5 *(Fig 113)*

1. Simple straddle vault with padded obstacle.
2. With springboard and safety mats, jump to handstand then drop flat.
3. From a stand on the horse, handspring to stand.
4. Horizontal astride vault to land on safety mats in a front support position.
5. With one leg leading, jump to a handstand with a quarter-turn.
6. From a stand 30cm (12in) from the wall, do 5 rebound jumps to touch the wall overhead.

Vaulting

Fig 114   Vault level 6.

Level 6 *(Fig 114)*

1.   Horizontal straddle, board a metre back, horse shoulder height.

2.   Horizontal squat.

3.   With horse and safety mats, handspring through handstand.

4.   Straight-leg squat.

5.   With springboard and safety mats, jump to a handstand with quarter-turn.

6.   Handspring vault, height midway between shoulder and hip.

8 Bar

LOW BAR *(Fig 115)*

Bar work is always the most spectacular of all the gymnastic events. Many spectators think that in some way the gymnast is fastened to the bar but of course this is not so. The only assistance which the gymnast has for the grip is a leather handguard which is there to help protect the hands. Girls work on a wooden bar whilst boys swing around a metal one. At the moment the girls' bar is oval but it is expected that over the next few years it will be adapted towards the smaller, round cross-section of the boys' bar. Bar work requires considerable strength in the shoulders and the arms to support the gymnast's weight and to raise and lower the body. In advanced gymnastics more than 75 per cent of the gymnast's time is spent using the hands to support the body-weight and so it is clear that much time must be spent conditioning for strength otherwise many movements will be impossible.

Always have your apparatus checked before the lesson starts and ensure that underneath the bar there is at least 160mm (6in) of mat, creating a soft surface. For young gymnasts a safety mat is a wise precaution. The bar should be set at about shoulder height to the gymnast. It is often

Fig 115   Drama. Gymnastics is a performing sport with expressive action and forms.

Bar

Fig 116   The low bar.

easier to adjust the height of the bar by adding or removing layers of mats rather than by altering the actual bar.

Fig 118   Undergrasp.

THE GRIPS *(Figs 117–119)*

Boys work on the smaller, round bar with a full grip, that is with the thumbs around the bar. Girls keep the thumb pressed in against the fingers. There are two types of grip which concern the young gymnast. The first is the overgrasp, when the back of the hands can be seen by the gymnast. The second is the undergrasp when the back of the hands face away from the gymnast. The gymnast can have one hand in overgrasp and one hang in undergrasp – this is called the combined grasp. There are other types of grip which are of little or no use to the novice

Fig 119   Combined grasp.

gymnast. Firstly the gymnast should learn to hang in each of these three grips. This may seem trivial, but a clear understanding of the grips is vital to avoid accidents.

Fig 117   Overgrasp.

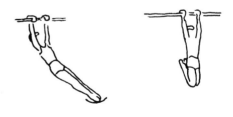

Fig 120   Overgrasp and undergrasp hang.

Fig 121 (a)–(h) A selection of hang positions.

THE HANG POSITIONS
(Figs 120–121)

The gymnast will build up strength and confidence during the first few weeks of training. It is easiest to begin by learning the hang positions under the bar, all in overgrasp.

(a) Straight Hang Either on a low bar with the feet resting forwards on the floor, or under supervision from a high bar.

(b) Hang with Bent Legs Either with the legs bent to the rear or with the legs bent to the front. Note that the ankles must be extended when clear of the floor.

(c) Tucked Hang with the knees held at shoulder height.

(d) Inverted Tuck The knees pull through the arms until the front of the foot touches the bar.

(e) Piked (horizontal) Hang with the legs held out parallel to the floor.

  Piked (vertical) Hang piked with the toes touching the bar.

(f) Inverted Pike Pull the feet between the hands then extend the legs to form a pike behind the bar.

(g) Back Hang Care must be taken with this hang position when very young children are training. Pull the feet through the hands and lower carefully down towards the floor. This will be familiar to some children as 'skin the cat'.

(h) Leg Acting Hang Pull one leg through the arms then hook it on to the bar. From the head to the extended leg the body should be a dished shape.

All of these hang positions may be practised in any of the grips, but must be static positions. Do not attempt to swing.

THE SUPPORT POSITIONS
(Fig 122)

There are three main support positions above the bar which once again can be practised in any of the grips. However, there must be a safety mat under the bar and

Bar

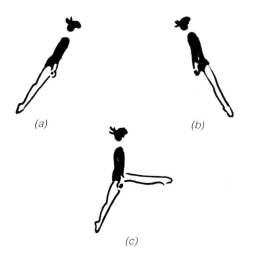

(a)

(b)

(c)

Fig 122 Support positions: (a) front support, (b) back support, and (c) split support.

there must be a coach to assist with balance. Falling backwards or forwards in the wrong grip will lead almost certainly to a fall.

(a) Front Support With the shoulders pressed down and the head up the bar will rest at the top of the thigh. The line from the shoulder to the foot will be straight.

(b) Back Support Once again with the shoulders pressed down and the head up, the bar rests at the back of the thigh. The gymnast does not sit on the bar – this is a position supported by the arms.

(c) Split Support This is in effect a front support position with one leg between the

arms and extended forwards. Lack of suppleness will make this position very uncomfortable to hold. Note that the bar touches the rear leg at the top of the thigh.

SWINGS

Basic Swing

There are two forms of basic swing to be learned. The swing is the first stage of learning to make circles around the bar and so it is very important. Remember that with all elements on the bar the gymnast is only as safe as the grip strength and the size of the hands, and so instruct to an appropriate degree of swing. Use safety mats at all times. All basic swings use overgrasp. Progress from a small swing to a large swing over several weeks. During this training the gymnast will begin to discover that the hands become a little sore. They may even blister. Take care in the first few sessions – a little often is a sure road to progress. Too much pain will make the bar unpopular.

Leg Acting Swing *(Fig 123)*

Start in the leg acting hang position. With a little assistance from the coach, the gymnast tightens the seat to pull the straight leg down to the floor. The head remains forwards and

must be overgrasp

Fig 123 Leg acting swing.

90

(a)

must be overgrasp

(b)

Fig 124 (a) and (b) Swing in hang.

the body in a dished shape on the return swing. In the same way that children on a playground swing will alter their shoulder position to build up swing, so too the gymnast will soon discover how to increase the leg acting swing. The arms at first will tend to bend when the shoulders rise but with experience they will remain straight.

Swing in Hang *(Fig 124)*

On a low bar it is not possible to swing straight as the gymnast passes under the bar and so the legs must bend under the bar.

On the forward swing the heels bend up to the seat and the hips lead the swing under the bar. The knees then pick up strongly into a tuck before extending upwards. The extension at the end of the swing carries the feet up and level with the bar.

On the return swing the back remains round with the knees drawing up before passing under the bar. This requires great effort from the gymnast to prevent the legs scraping along the floor.

The swing will commence from a hang under the bar with the gymnast attempting to make the correct shapes. As already seen with the leg acting swing the gymnast will learn through experience how to increase the movement. The coach, however, must always be on hand to check the shape and to ensure that on the back swing the hands do not loosen their grip of the bar. The return swing always requires the greatest attention. If the gymnast can see the bar then the

must be overgrasp

Fig 125   Leg acting upstart.

position will be more secure. Never hollow on the back swing – this will make the grip less secure.

SKILLS INTO SUPPORT

Leg Acting Upstart *(Fig 125)*

Having already learned to swing in the leg acting position the gymnast can now use this experience to make a swing into support. The leg acting upstart is an extension of the leg acting swing. To start with the gymnast must make a large leg acting swing and learn to pull the shoulders forward and above the bar. Do not expect this to be done with straight arms immediately. Allow the gymnast to find the position by pulling into then pressing above the bar. Once a good rhythm of swing is found the gymnast will soon be able to rise on straight arms into a

split support. The grip will change from hang to support by rolling the hands around the bar. This shifting of the wrists is very important.

Upward Circle *(Fig 126)*

Begin with the bar at shoulder height. Stand facing the bar holding it in overgrasp with straight arms. Bend the arms and pull the shoulders to the bar. Keeping the arms bent, pull the knees up towards the bar to form a tuck shape. As soon as the feet leave the ground a small swing will start and the shoulders will pass under the bar. As they swing under, the gymnast places the hips on the bar, still retaining a tuck. When all of the weight is above the bar, the arms can be straightened up into front support. If the gymnast starts with the feet placed immediately under the bar then much more strength is required. The upward circle can be assisted by a

Fig 126   (a)–(f)   Upward circle progressions.

coach or by self-help, pushing off a rolled-up mat or a padded box top. Once learned with bent arms and legs the gymnast can progress to straight legs and eventually (and very much more difficultly) with straight arms.

Bar

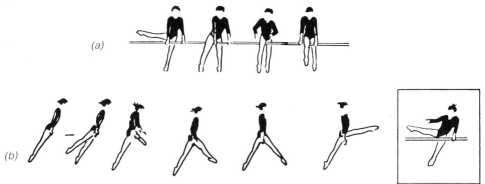

(a)

(b)

Fig 127 (a) and (b) Front support to split support.

Changing Support

The ability to change from one support to another will be required to make up simple bar exercises. All of the following changes start and end in overgrasp. It is almost always the hands which carry the gymnast's weight, but there is a momentary checking of the balance in the first and the simplest of these movements.

Front Support to Split Support
(Fig 127)

(a)   From a front support, raise one leg to the side and pass it over the bar whilst moving the hips to the side of the support position. Rest the forward leg on the bar and then release the bar with both hands and regrasp either side of the forward leg.
(b)   From a front support, lean to one side and lift the opposite leg up and over the bar. With the weight now transferred to one arm it is possible to release with one hand and regrasp after the leg has arrived at the front.

From Split Support to Back Support
(Fig 128)

Holding the hips well forward, lean to the side and take all the weight on one arm, releasing the other to allow the rear leg to lift

Fig 128   Split support into back support.

over the bar. The shoulders move back as both legs join together in back support.

From Back Support to Front Support
(Fig 129)

This is a tricky combination. The gymnast leans back and to the side to carry the weight on one arm. With the feet together, one arm lifts and the body rolls sideways to regrasp in front support. Do not leave the feet behind when turning. With a straight body, the entire length of the shape is turned at the same time.

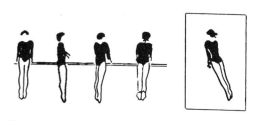

Fig 129   From back support to front support.

From Split Support Half-Turn to Front Support *(Fig 130)*

The lean is combined with a half-turn as the gymnast reaches. To turn to the left, lean first to the right and change the left hand to undergrasp. Then lean to the left and as the right leg lifts over the bar make a half-turn by reaching across the body to regrasp in front support.

Fig 130   *From split support, half-turn to front support.*

BACKWARD MILL CIRCLE 1 (Leg Acting) *(Fig 131)*

(a)   Begin in split support with the hands in overgrasp. Lift the hips upwards and backwards, hooking the front leg on to the bar.
(b)   Reach out and back with the shoulders to swing down and under the bar. The straight leg pikes in towards the bar to assist with the swing.
(c)   Shift the wrists up on top of the bar and correct the position to a good split support once more.

BACKWARD MILL CIRCLE 2 (Straight Legs) *(Fig 132)*

This is performed with straight legs throughout and is considerably more difficult. From split support the shoulders lift up and back and the leading leg rises towards a vertical line before the circle starts. The bar is pressed against the rear leg at all times. The circle is much slower to rise into support and requires courage to maintain position. The assistance of a coach for this skill is essential. The coach helps to complete the lift into the support.

Fig 131   *Backward mill circle with leg acting.*

Fig 132   *Backward mill circle with straight legs.*

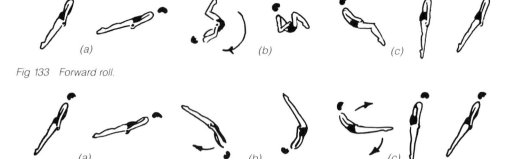

Fig 133 Forward roll.

Fig 134 Forward roll with pike under bar.

BACKWARD ROLL *(Fig 135)*

This is also known as the backward hip circle as the hips remain close to the bar. Once again it is an advanced skill in the beginner's repertoire and will require the assistance of a coach.

(a) The movement starts with a layaway from the bar, gaining height and momentum for the roll. With a small bend of the arms the bar is placed on the waist and the feet pike under the bar. The heels then swing up and back and the arms push straight, lifting the gymnast clear of the bar.
(b) With a straight body the hips are returned towards the bar.
(c) The shoulders fall back and with a dished body shape the gymnast circles under the bar. Note that the head remains slightly forward.
(d) The wrists shift up into support and the gymnast, with the assistance of the coach, lifts the shoulders up maintaining a straight body.

FORWARD ROLL
(Figs 133–134)

This is probably the most difficult skill in the starter's handbook of gymnastics.

(a) Start in overgrasp. From a straight front support position lean forwards and begin to fall forwards. Ensure that the heels and the legs are not left behind.
(b) When the body has passed a horizontal position round the back, reach under and up with the shoulders and at the same time pull the heel on to the seat. This will form a tuck as the body rolls under the bar.
(c) As you rise shift the wrists into a strong support and straighten the body out.

Do not tuck until the shoulders are below bar height. The same forward roll can be made with a pike under the bar (Fig 134).

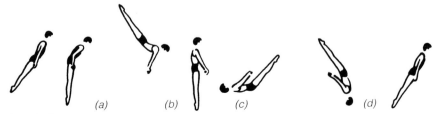

Fig 135 Backward roll.

DISMOUNTS

Essential to all dismounts is the ability to make a layaway from the bar. This layaway is made in overgrasp from a front support by making a small pike under the bar then swinging the legs and the hips up and away towards a handstand. Notice how the shoulders come forward as the initial pike is formed to balance the body on the bar (Fig 136).

This skill will develop with strength, and strength will develop with experience on the apparatus. Dismounts will therefore tend to be mastered later than the other bar skills.

Layaway Dismounts
(Figs 137–141)

The simplest dismount to perform is a straight layaway from the bar (Fig 137). At the height of the swing the gymnast pushes away from the bar to land facing it.

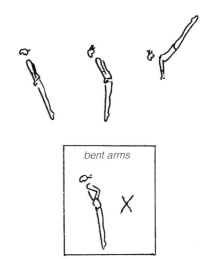

bent arms

Fig 136   Initial pike for layaway dismount.

More interesting but more difficult to land, is the layaway dismount with a half-turn (Fig 138). Here a half-turn is introduced at the height of the backward swing. For a moment the gymnast will have just one hand on the

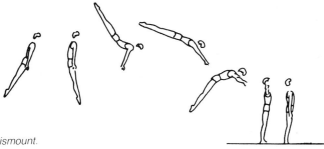

Fig 137   Layaway dismount.

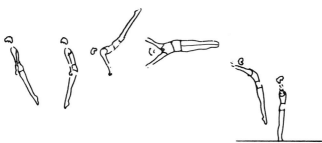

Fig 138   Layaway dismount with half-turn.

bar, pressing away strongly through the supporting arm. After the release, the turn is completed to land facing away from the bar.

To build awareness of the correct shape and strength, start in a straight hang under the bar and then lower to a held dish shape (Fig 139). The assistance of a coach is vital to shaping and supporting the undershoot in the learning stages (Fig 140). There is no single way to support, but ensure that whichever method is used the coach gives the assistance required to complete the skill. At times two supporters may be necessary.

Seen from the side in Fig 141 the co-ordination required between the use of the shapes and the pull-down on the bar can be identified. The legs and the hips are set very high before the shoulders swing upwards and the arch is introduced.

Underbar Dismounts
(Fig 142)

The undershoot or underswing is a very important dismount requiring great understanding of shape and strength to hold the position during swing.

The simple undershoot is made from a layaway above the bar (Fig 142 (a)). As the body swings towards a front support the head is held forward. A gap is left between the hips and the bar by trying to place the upper thigh against the bar. The back must be kept in a dished shape. This is retained as the swing passes under the bar. Only when the shoulders begin to rise up the other side of the bar is the dished shape released to form an arched shape. To assist with the lift, the arms pull the bar down towards the floor before release. The head

Fig 139   Layaway dismount progression.

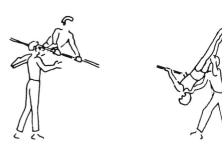

Fig 140   Support for layaway dismount.

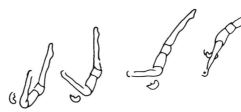

Fig 141   The correct shapes for the layaway dismount.

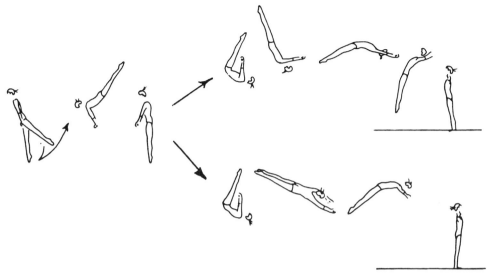

Fig 142 (a) Undershoot dismount, and (b) undershoot dismount with half-turn.

falls back in flight and comes forward again for the recovery and the landing. The addition of a half-turn can be made in the arching stage of the dismount (Fig 142 (b)).

The most common error with the undershoot will be incorrect placing of the hips. Either they will rest on the bar or they will be allowed to fall away from the bar until the feet are touching. Both these errors will prevent the undershoot from gaining any height. There is also a tendency for young gymnasts to pull too early into a hollow shape rather than make a late pull from a dished shape.

Straddle Sole Circle Dismount

As shown in Fig 144 (e), this dismount requires the gymnast to make a three-quarter circle under and around the bar to dismount with a jump from the bar.

From the layaway bring the feet into a straddle stand on the bar. Press the head down on to the chest and with the weight

held on the hands and the feet fall to pass under the bar. As the swing carries you up the other side lift the head and transfer the weight on to the feet so that the hands can release the grip. From a stand, stretch jump off to dismount.

Fig 143 Straddle sole circle dismount with support.

Bar

Over the Bar Dismounts
(Fig 144 (a–d))

(a) *Squat on and jump off.* A simple squat-on from the layaway allows the gymnast to stand up and stretch jump off the bar.

(b) *Through vault* (tucked squat). From the layaway there must be a vault-like thrust from the bar to lift the hips.

(c) *Squat-on or through vault with straight legs.* These are more advanced shapes than before requiring a sharper contrast of shapes and actions.

(d) *Layaway to straddle stand and jump off or straddle vault off the bar.* This requires more courage than before but makes for an attractive dismount.

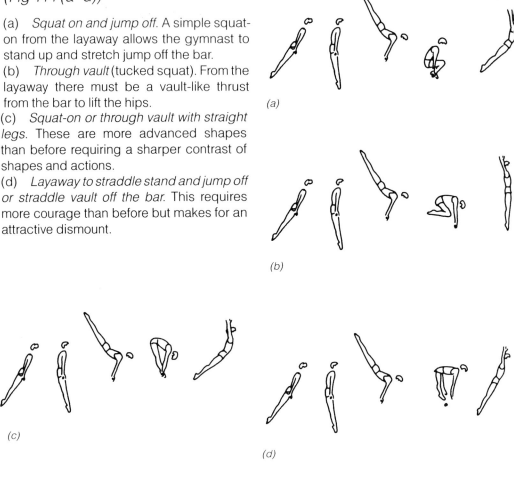

(a)

(b)

(c)

(d)

(e)

Fig 144 (a)–(e) Over the bar and straddle sole circle dismounts.

1.

2.

3.

4.

Fig 145   Bar exercise 1.

BAR EXERCISES

Bar Exercise 1 *(Fig 145)*

On a single low bar an exercise for a boy will vary very little from an exercise for a girl. The skills are identical and the combinations are limited. The exercise begins in overgrasp.

1.   From a stand, pull to the bar and make an upward circle with straight legs.
2.   Lift the right leg over the bar to a split support.
3.   Drop back and make a leg acting upstart.
4.   Change the right hand to undergrasp and lifting the left leg up and over the bar, make a half-turn to dismount.

Bar

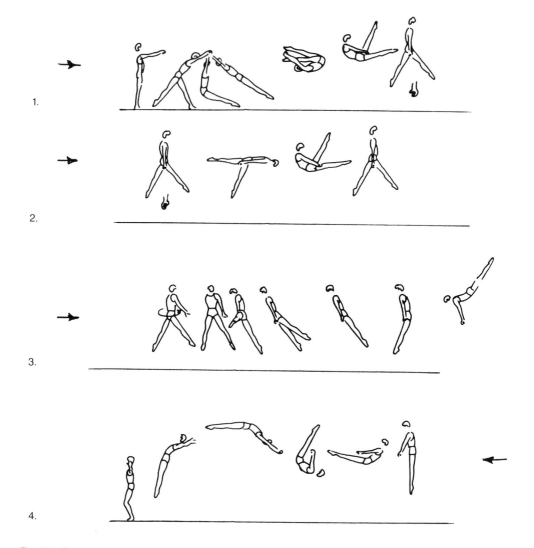

1.

2.

3.

4.

Fig 146   Bar exercise 2.

Bar Exercise 2 *(Fig 146)*

This exercise begins in overgrasp.

1.   From a stand, pike swing through and pull one leg through the hands to make a straight leg acting upstart into a split support.

2.   Change both hands to undergrasp and make a forward mill circle.

3.   Make a half-turn across the bar to a front support in overgrasp.

4.   From a short layaway, undershoot dismount to a stand.

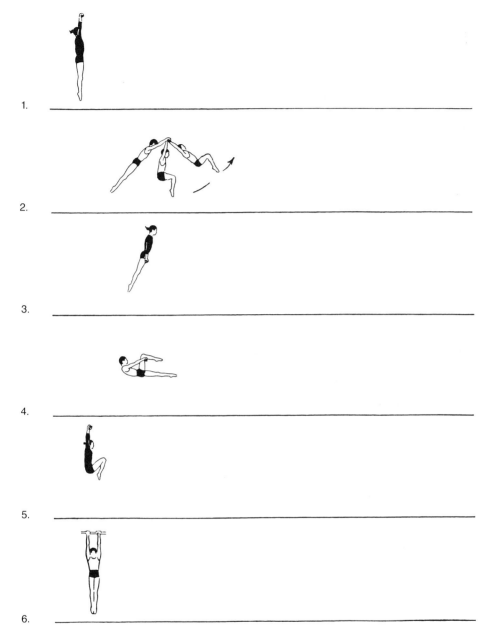

1. _____

2. _____

3. _____

4. _____

5. _____

6. _____

Fig 147   Bar level 1.

BAR SKILLS

Bar Level 1 *(Fig 147)*

1. Simple hang.
2. Swing with knees bent.
3. Front support.
4. Leg acting position.
5. Hang with a tuck.
6. Hang in combined grasp.

Bar

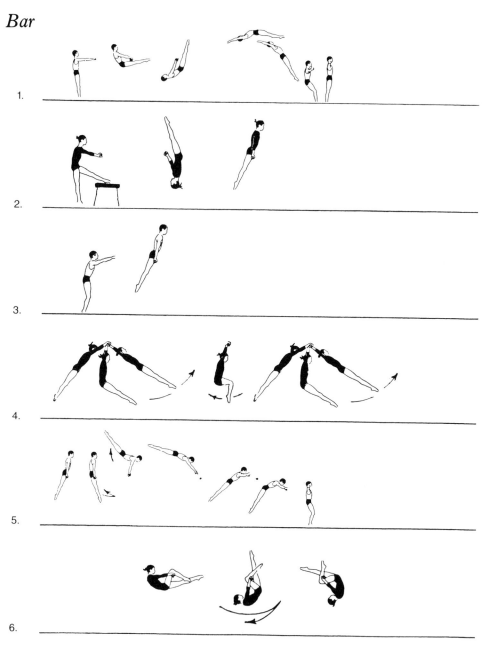

1.

2.

3.

4.

5.

6.

Fig 148   Bar level 2.

Bar Level 2 (Fig 148)

1. Undershoot from stand.
2. Upward circle (using a box top).
3. Jump to support.

4. 3 swings with legs extending.
5. From support, push off to stand.
6. Leg acting swing.

Fig 149 Bar level 3.

Bar Level 3 *(Fig 149)*

1. From hang, 3 chins to the bar.
2. From front support, beat off the bar, returning to support.
3. In undergrasp, forward mill circle.
4. From astride support in overgrasp, drop back and leg acting upstart.
5. Piked inverted hang.
6. From astride support, release one hand and make a half-turn to front support.

Bar

1. _____

2. _____

3. _____

4. _____

5. _____

6. _____

Fig 150 Bar level 4.

Bar Level 4 (Fig 150)

1. Pass one leg over the bar to astride support.
2. Back mill circle, leg acting (overgrasp).
3. Back support.
4. Upward circle.
5. Hang, tuck, straighten legs and lower.
6. Swing half-turn to combined grasp and dismount.

Fig 151   Bar level 5.

Bar Level 5 *(Fig 151)*

1. Backward roll.
2. Layaway to one-leg squat.
3. From hang lift legs to straddle and sit on lower bar . (Asymmetric bars).
4. From astride support, swing leg over the bar backwards to catch in front support.
5. Simple through vault over a single low bar.
6. Piked and straddled inverted hang.

Bar

1.

2.

3.

4.

5.

6.

Fig 152   Bar level 6.

Bar Level 6 (Fig 152)

1. Undershoot dismount.
2. Squat both legs to back support.
3. From astride support, drop back into straight single leg upstart.
4. From hang, with straight legs squat to piked inverted hang.
5. Swing with half-turn to swing.
6. Backward mill circle (overgrasp).

9 Beam

Of all the gymnastics apparatus the beam is the easiest to construct an exercise for at beginner level. However, at advanced level it is the most difficult apparatus on which to perform. Its full name is the balance beam and as the name implies it is a test of balance. Simple dance steps, leaps, rolls and jumps are combined to make a short exercise which moves along the beam before dismounting. In recent years the basic floor agilities have been added but these are mainly for the more experienced gymnasts.

To begin with, much work has to be done to ensure a fine sense of balance, first by performing on benches with a wide surface, then on narrower platforms until the beam is mastered at floor level. A little at a time the beam can then be raised until it is well clear of the floor. Do not be in a great hurry. Just because a forward roll seems easy on a bench it doesn't follow that it will be easy on the beam. It is surprising just how much the sense of balance changes with height. It is also important to make the learning stages safe. A fall will do little for the confidence. And before looking at the first lesson one more reminder: 'It's not what you do it's the way that you do it.' Style, shape and form mean everything in gymnastics.

LEARNING TO BALANCE

Now that we know what balance is and now that we realise that everyone has the ability to balance, we are in a position to exercise that skill and refine it.

Stand with the feet apart and follow a series of simple arm placements as shown in Fig 154 (overleaf). Now repeat the actions with the feet together and with the eyes closed. At all times hold the head up and keep the shoulders down. If the balance is

Fig 153 Concentration. Accuracy and timing are essential for the safe performance of gymnastics skills. In a competition a gymnast will focus many years of work into a routine lasting less than a minute.

Beam

(a)

(b)

Fig 154 (a) and (b) Balance exercises.

failing stop the arms moving and try to adjust the stance to retain stability.

Repeat this exercise standing at the end of a bench. Look at a fixed point and concentrate. Try to be very conscious of the contact with the bench. Try to picture the bench underneath and behind you. Your 'mind's eye' is a valuable tool to aid skill and balance. Your mind already has the information, it has been collecting it. You must try to use it by being aware of it.

SIMPLE WALKING

Balance has already been defined and identified. Now that sense of balance must be put to the test with more difficult forms of movement. Control and posture should be considered at all times. Perhaps the single most common fault at this level results from the misconception that arriving at the other end of the bench is the main goal of the exercise, and that children are 'getting along fine' with a little run towards the end. It is quality of movement and the increased awareness of arm positions, shoulders, head and so on that are vital.

Forwards (Fig 155 (a))

Start from a stand at the end of the bench. Raise the arms to the side with the shoulders held down and the head up. Walk slowly to the other end. Now walk up on the toes.

Sideways (Fig 155 (b))

This is a side-step with the arms raised and the head facing to the side. Now walk up on the toes.

Backwards (Fig 155 (c))

Once again with the upper body fixed, lift one leg from the bench and, keeping it straight, slide it along the edge of the bench and place it to the rear. Now walk up on the toes.

With Arms Changing (Fig 156)

Use the arm movements from the first balance exercise to add to these simple walking skills. The changes of arm position should follow a gentle transition from shape to shape and the speed must be in time with the walk. Keep the shoulders down and the head up. Relax the hands and walk up on the toes.

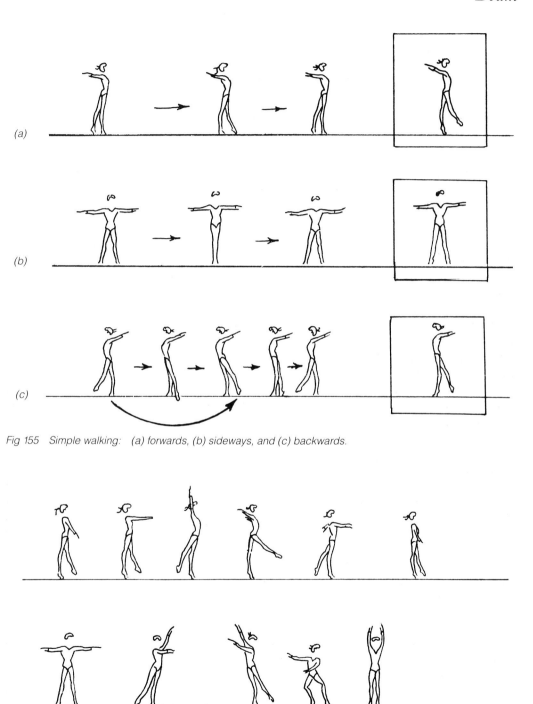

Fig 155   Simple walking: (a) forwards, (b) sideways, and (c) backwards.

Fig 156   Simple walking with arms changing.

Beam

JUMPS *(Figs 157–158)*

Jumps can be made on the bench or beam. For these a new position for the feet is required. Move one foot forward until the heel and the toe are in line. Once on the beam the feet will have to be one in front of the other almost in line. Jumps are made in a very similar way to the method of jumping already found for floor and vaulting. The shoulders must not be allowed to lean outside the line of the feet. Place the weight equally on both legs. From a small bend of the legs, the arms are drawn down and back. The arms swing forwards and upwards and the legs extend, pushing through the seat and the ankles for maximum effort. The landing is made by gently taking the weight on a small bend of the legs, and the balance is checked by opening the arms. There are three main parts to every jump:

1. Height, reached by the power of the jump.
2. Shape, which defines the type of jump.
3. Recovery and balance, for stability.

Study each shape and pay special attention to a full extension of the ankles after leaving the beam.

Fig 157   Jumping.

Fig 158   Jumps.

LEAPS *(Figs 159–160)*

While jumps come from two feet, leaps take their power from just one leg. Most leaps have split leg shapes or have turns in them. The gymnast can walk slowly into leaps, gaining height from the extra momentum, or even take a short run. But this advantage can also cause problems with balance since the leaps are then much more difficult to recover from. The landing will still require the leg to bend for a gentle recovery. The simplest of the leaps is from one foot to the other with the arms at shoulder height.

Fig 159   Leaps.

land left   *land right*

with half-turn, land right   *land right*

Fig 160   Leaps, all right leg take-off.

MOUNTS AND DISMOUNTS

Once simple movements can be made by walking along the bench, different ways of getting on and off the apparatus should be taught. These are mounts and dismounts.

Dismounts *(Fig 161)*

(a)   From a stand at the end of the bench use any of the jumps from the floorwork and vaulting sections, for example the stretch jump, the tuck jump, the straddle jump or the astride jump.
(b)   Arab-spring.

Mounts for Bench and Low Beam *(Fig 162)*

(a)   From a stand on the floor, raise the arms and step up to another stand.
(b)   Using a springboard, from a short run stretch jump to a stand.
(c)   Walk forwards and swing one leg up. Leap to land on one leg, holding the rear leg up.
(d)   Using a springboard, from a short run tuck jump to land on the bench.

Fig 161   (a) and (b)   Dismounts.

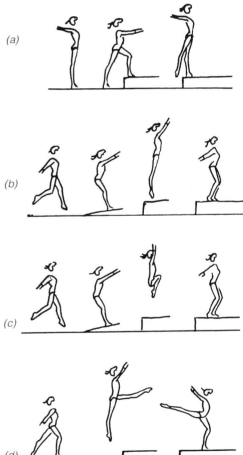

Fig 162   (a)–(d)   Mounts for bench and low beam.

Mounts for High Beam
(Fig 163)

(a) From a stand facing the side of the beam, place the hands on the beam and push up to a front support. Lift one leg over the beam to a split support and turn to sit side-saddle. Turn to straddle sit then swing the legs back to place the feet to the rear. Lift the seat, place one foot on the beam and stand up.

(b) Using a springboard, stand sideways to the beam and scissor kick to sit in a straddle position. Reach forwards to a front lie then push back on to one knee before stepping up to a stand.

(a)

(b)

Fig 163 (a) and (b) Mounts for high beam.

TURNS AND SPINS

Half-Turn, High on Both Feet
(Fig 164)

Start with the head up and the shoulders back. The arms should be extended sideways for maximum balance. Rise on to the toes, raise the arms above the head and keep the seat tight. Use the feet to initiate the turn. Lower arms sideways to aid balance.

Fig 164 Half-turn, high on both feet.

Half-Spin, High on One Foot
(Fig 165)

Step forward and rise on to the ball of the foot with the arms lifting to an extended position above the head. The spin is initiated from the shoulders and the hips with the trailing leg bending to tuck in behind the support leg. The arms lower to the side. It can be carried to a single leg recovery and balance.

Half-Turn, Low on Both Feet
(Fig 166)

Note the upright head and back position. The feet initiate the turn, keeping a fixed shape throughout. It will be difficult here to maintain a fixed upper body posture.

Half or Full Spin, Low on One Foot *(Fig 167)*

From a deep forward lunge, this spin is initiated by the arm and the shoulder. First hold the arms to the same side as the rear leg. Now by swinging them across at shoulder height the spin will carry the rear leg around to the same lunge position on the opposite side. This can be extended to make a full turn.

Fig 165   Half-spin, high on one foot.

Fig 166   Half-turn, low on both feet.

Fig 167   Half or full spin, low on one foot.

Fig 168   A beam exercise.

A BEAM EXERCISE *(Fig 168)*

1. From a short run, leap to a stand.
2. Hop–step hop–step, stand, rise and half-turn.
3. Stretch jump with forward travel to crouch, then to another stretch jump and crouch, ending in a half-turn and stand.
4. From a side stand, side body wave into a stand.
5. Step forward and cart-wheel dismount.

Beam

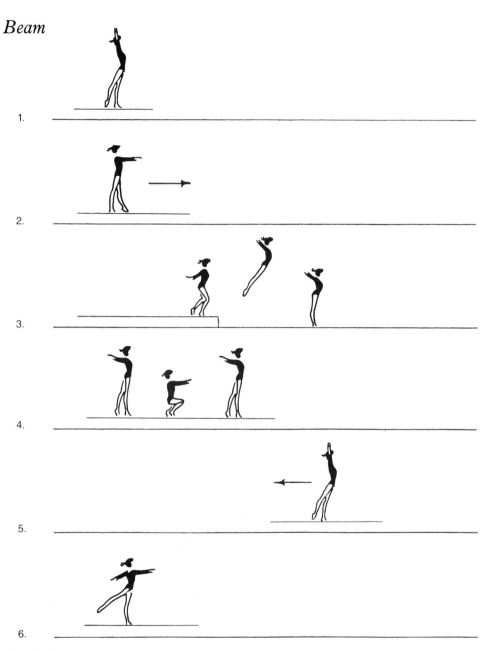

1.

2.

3.

4.

5.

6.

Fig 169   Beam level 1.

BEAM SKILLS

Beam Level 1 *(Fig 169)*

1. Simple stand in balance.
2. Walk forward with good posture.
3. Stretch jump from the end.
4. Squat down and stand up.
5. Walk back three steps.
6. Balance on one foot.

Fig 170 Beam level 2.

Beam Level 2 *(Fig 170)*

1. Pivot on the toes.
2. Forward roll.
3. Stretch jump on.
4. Arabesque.
5. Spring with leg changes.
6. Walk with arms changing position.

Beam

1.

2.

3.

4.

5.

6.

Fig 171   Beam level 3.

Beam Level 3 *(Fig 171)*

1. Splits.
2. Backward roll.
3. Tuck jump.

4. Cart-wheel.
5. Squat and half-turn.

Beam 0.5 metres

6. Squat on.

Fig 172   Beam level 4.

Beam Level 4 *(Fig 172)*

1. Push to bridge.
2. Dance combination.
3. From back lie, with hands clear of the bench, tuck and roll forward to stand.
4. 3 consecutive but different jumps.

Beam 1 metre

5. On the toes, half-turn.
6. Round-off dismount.

Beam

1.

2.

3.

4.

5.

6.

Fig 173   Beam level 5.

Beam Level 5 *(Fig 173)*

1.   Kick to handstand.
2.   Hold V-sit.
3.   Jump with foot exchanges.

Beam 1 metre

4.   Arabesque.
5.   Mount, squat on.
6.   Dismount, stretch jump.

1. _____

2. _____

3. _____

4. _____

5. _____

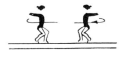

6. _____

Fig 174 Beam level 6.

Beam Level 6 *(Fig 174)*

Beam 1 metre
1. Held V-sit.
2. 2 consecutive springs.
3. Mount, single leg squat.
4. 2 consecutive hops.
5. Hold straddle support.
6. Squat and half-turn.

Index